*Inter* te(X)t

The La... of W...

'This book ...
a measured ...
language, a ...
reader, as t...

The INTE... ... T ... es has be... ... designed ... meet the needs ...
contempo... ... nglish Language Studies. ... ... *cor* (in...
duction to ... ... se analysis *text* and routine ...(2001) ... the foundation tex...
which is c... ... ... a ... ge of ... ... write student...
with hand... ... ... experience of ... ... pic...
and can b... ... ... or in ... ...

The Langu... ... Websites

◎   expl... ... way in which ... ... language

◎   cove... ... ... website ... ...
     histo... ... and media persp... ...

◎   cons... ... how the W... ... ... and ... ...
     has ... ...
     tradi... ...

◎   featu... ... ...
     inclu... ... ... ICT ... ...

◎   is ac... ... ...

Mark Boa... ... ... Head of ... ... Keighley, York-
shire, UK. ... is an experienced teacher, having taught Advanced English
Language, English Literature and Media Studies for many years and has been
a Senior Examiner. He also founded and runs The English Language List, an
email discussion and support group for teachers of English Language.

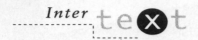

The Intertext series

The Routledge INTERTEXT series aims to develop readers' understanding of how texts work. It does this by showing some of the designs and patterns in the language from which they are made, by placing texts within the contexts in which they occur, and by exploring relationships between them.

The series consists of a foundation text, *Working with Texts: A core introduction to language analysis*, which looks at language aspects essential for the analysis of texts, and a range of satellite texts. These apply aspects of language to a particular topic area in more detail. They complement the core text and can also be used alone, providing the user has the foundation skills furnished by the core text.

Benefits of using this series:

◎　**Multi-disciplinary** – provides a foundation for the analysis of texts, supporting students who want to achieve a detailed focus on language.

◎　**Accessible** – no previous knowledge of language analysis is assumed, just an interest in language use.

◎　**Student-friendly** – contains activities relating to texts studied, commentaries after activities, highlighted key terms, suggestions for further reading and an index of terms.

◎　**Interactive** – offers a range of task-based activities for both class use and self-study.

◎　**Tried and tested** – written by a team of respected teachers and practitioners whose ideas and activities have been trialled independently.

The series editors:

Adrian Beard was until recently Head of English at Gosforth High School, and now works at the University of Newcastle upon Tyne. He is a Chief Examiner for AS and A Level English Literature. He has written and lectured extensively on the subjects of literature and language. His publications include *Texts and Contexts* (Routledge).

Angela Goddard is Head of Programme for Language and Human Communication at the University College of York St John, and is Chair of Examiners for A Level English Language. Her publications include *Researching Language* (second edition, Heinemann, 2000).

Core textbook:

Working with Texts: A core introduction to language analysis
(second edition, 2001)
Ronald Carter, Angela Goddard, Danuta Reah, Keith Sanger and
Maggie Bowring

Satellite titles:

The Language of Advertising: Written texts
(second edition, 2002)
Angela Goddard

Language Change
Adrian Beard

The Language of Children
Julia Gillen

The Language of Comics
Mario Saraceni

The Language of Conversation
Francesca Pridham

The Language of Drama
Keith Sanger

The Language of Fiction
Keith Sanger

Language and Gender
Angela Goddard and Lindsey Meân
Patterson

The Language of Humour
Alison Ross

The Language of ICT: Information and communication technology
Tim Shortis

The Language of Magazines
Linda McLoughlin

The Language of Newspapers
(second edition, 2002)
Danuta Reah

The Language of Poetry
John McRae

The Language of Politics
Adrian Beard

The Language of Speech and Writing
Sandra Cornbleet and
Ronald Carter

The Language of Sport
Adrian Beard

The Language of Television
Jill Marshall and Angela Werndly

The Language of Websites
Mark Boardman

The Language of Work
Almut Koester

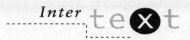

The Language of Websites

◎   Mark Boardman

Routledge
Taylor & Francis Group

LONDON AND NEW YORK

First published 2005
by Routledge
2 Park Square, Milton Park, Abingdon, Oxon OX14 4RN

Simultaneously published in the USA and Canada
by Routledge
270 Madison Ave, New York, NY 10016

Routledge is an imprint of the Taylor & Francis Group

© 2005 Mark Boardman

Typeset in Stone Sans/Stone Serif by
Florence Production Ltd, Stoodleigh, Devon
Printed and bound in Great Britain by
TJ International Ltd, Padstow, Cornwall

British Library Cataloguing in Publication Data
A catalogue record for this book is available from the
British Library

Library of Congress Cataloging in Publication Data
Boardman, Mark, 1961–
    The language of websites/Mark Boardman.
        p. cm. – (The intertext series)
    Includes bibliographical references and indexes.
    1. Web sites. 2. World Wide Web. 3. English language – Usage.
    I. Title. II. Series: Intertext (London, England)
    TK5105.888.B62 2004
    025.04'014 – dc 22   2004007127

ISBN 0–415–32853–5 (hbk)
ISBN 0–415–32854–3 (pbk)

This book is for Judith, Gemma and Lisa –
the power of three . . .

contents

acknowledgements

My thanks to Angela Goddard for making the initial suggestion that I have a go at writing this book – thereby implying that I might be up to the task – and for her support in the early stages of writing. I am similarly grateful to Tim Shortis for help with secondary sources and his positive comments. Thanks also to Christy Kirkpatrick for her support and patience in the early stages of writing. Kate Parker's support, patience and understanding have been very much appreciated throughout the writing process. I am highly indebted to Adrian Beard for his enthusiastic and insightful editorial guidance.

I also appreciated the encouraging comments made by staff and students at South Craven School while I was trying to balance writing with teaching.

I am very grateful to the following people and organisations for their kind permission to let me use screenshots from their websites in this book: Nick Reynolds (joint lead vocalist of Foruta), Anthony Coxar, Matt Wells (creator of Gigablast), Chuck Olsen, Mon Athakravi, Hank Lake Coghlan (of Lake Coghlan – IT & Marketing for Business & Law), Salford University, AltaVista Operations Ltd, Footprint Films (Text 9 designed by Franki & Jonny) and Telegraph.co.uk, the website for the *Daily Telegraph* and the *Sunday Telegraph*.

conventions

Throughout this book, the convention of quoting a website address with the http:// prefix has been used. Modern web browsers no longer require this. It is preserved here because it gives a better understanding of the kind of document you are loading when you look at a web page. You also still need to include the prefix if you are making links as a writer of web pages – because there is more than one kind of link.

The Index of terms gives a short explanation of each special term, with the page number where it is first used. Each term is **emboldened** on its first mention only.

There's a lot to be said for being able to sit at a terminal and just dream.

(Tim Berners-Lee)

Bedrooms lack the potentially global bandwidth of homepages on the Web.

(Daniel Chandler and Dilwyn Roberts-Young)

introduction

Some background to language and the Web

Analysing a **text** is not an end in itself, although it may often seem that way if you have to do it under exam conditions. By separating out acts of communication and calling them texts, we hope to gain a better understanding of human communication. Additionally, in the electronic age, there is a problem with defining texts as either written or spoken. A **website** is a particular kind of electronic text that is technologically and culturally related to some aspects of written communication, but websites also have a relationship with spoken interaction and with other forms of electronic text. The technological and cultural factors that led to the appearance of websites are complex, but it would be wrong to attempt a linguistic analysis of websites in a vacuum.

How the **personal computer** (PC) came to be, and how this development dovetailed with the appearance of the Web, are crucial contextual factors in understanding how websites work as cultural artefacts. The context of websites is technologically determined. Much of the context of spoken and written interaction relies on a common sense awareness of the world around you. This is not so with websites: you cannot intuitively know how a computer displays web pages. For this reason, the introduction will provide some historical and technical background, which will be continued in Unit one, with a more specific focus on using language and media/communication studies **frameworks** for analysing web text.

1

Text analysis is a description of the process of reading – and in the case of websites the texts can only be read in an essentially fragile, technologically defined environment. That environment, or more specifically, the reader's awareness of its fragility, is a key factor in the reading process. This book sets out partly to show you the nature of the technologically defined space that is the context of web reading, so you will have to read through some technical background before you get to the analysis of texts. Technical explanations have generally been kept as simple as possible – but some technical material is needed in order to see how language interfaces with technology. Technology *is* the physical context of the Web, so it needs to be described. To leave it out would be like analysing a conversation without knowing the situation in which the conversation took place.

Any terminology that is given a full explanation in the glossary at the back of the book will appear in bold print the first time it is used. Because of the nature of the Web, the terminology is necessarily a mixture of technological, linguistic and media/communication studies terminology. Also, because this is an interdisciplinary book attempting an approach based on a combination of linguistic, ICT, media/communication studies and, occasionally, literary frameworks, it is a big glossary – larger than the glossaries in most other Intertext titles. The only real assumption the book makes is that the reader is aware of basic word classes – noun, verb, adjective, adverb, determiner, preposition and conjunction. For an approachable handbook that unlocks most of the grammatical mysteries an advanced or undergraduate student would ever encounter, you cannot do much better than David Crystal's (1998) *Rediscover Grammar*.

WHAT THE BOOK IS NOT

The activities in the book are essentially jumping-off points for any number of possible paths that could be taken when looking into the complex ways in which the interface between language and technology works. The commentaries highlight *some* of the possible avenues of investigation suggested by the activities, and also attempt to exemplify a workable linguistic methodology – but the commentaries are definitely not 'answers' to the questions in any kind of closed-off, complete sense. There is no *single* answer to a text analysis question, so if your response to the activity is different from the commentary this should not be seen as a problem. The Intertext series is all about raising your game as an analyser of texts on language-, media- or communication studies-based courses at advanced and first-year undergraduate level. If you can imitate the style and approach of the commentaries in this book, your game will be raised. The commentaries work by exemplifying an approach, a methodology – *not* by providing 'tick-box', neatly packaged 'answers'.

Similarly, the book suggests a few areas that could be developed by further academic research at higher education level, but it is not making claims to be definitive or exhaustive academically. For example, some of the analysis in this book hinges on the idea of **narrative** as the driving force behind the Web and how it works as a form of communication. This book is too small to pursue all the issues raised by the connection between narrative and the Web – but if you are interested in knowing more about this area (a well-established one academically), there is plenty of further reading in the bibliography.

HUMAN COMMUNICATION

We need to represent ourselves. We need to record our lives. Whatever you decide was the original purpose of cave paintings, it is at least clear that they show a human desire to make a long-term record of human activities. No other species on the planet seems to do this.

Another capability that separates us from other species is language. Chimpanzees can be taught some lexical knowledge, but they are incapable of handling the grammatical, **semantic** and **pragmatic** relations that are the true foundations of human language – and humans are alone in possessing a sophisticated vocal tract. Once we had language, we could go beyond pictures and begin to connect events with a system that has come to be known as narrative. We could now learn not only from our own experience, but also by listening to the experiences of others. The device used to store these experiences and narratives is the human brain – far from infallible, and even now very far from being perfectly understood. But each individual has a brain that is unreliable in slightly *different* ways, unique to them. So, if you send ten people to the same meeting or the same football match or the same party, you will get ten different spoken accounts of that event afterwards.

The storage and retrieval systems that the brain uses are imperfect, and we subconsciously fill in invented details when we cannot remember the actual details, because we wish to sound fluent when recounting an event. Add to this the infinite flexibility of language – choosing a word, choosing the order of the words, choosing features like **pitch**, **intonation** and pragmatic meaning – and you have a planet resonating with millions of unique spoken narratives every second of every day. This has been so since human language began. A good storyteller is someone who has trained their storage and retrieval system to hold more information than average, can retrieve information quickly and can then construct narratives that satisfy and entertain. Cultures are built upon how we respond to the interplay of these narratives – old ones and constantly changing new ones.

As our lives became more complex, we felt the need to fix these narratives in a form that could be replayed without variation and without error – to fix and record our culture and later to make the recordings themselves into cultural artefacts with **conventions** of their own. The only evidence of fixed narratives from the hunter-gatherer phase in our evolution comes from cave paintings – the precise purpose of which remains unknown. There may have been a predictable, culturally defined way of decoding them into spoken language, but this too will never be known.

It is because of the change from hunter-gatherer to farmer that we see social groups becoming less geographically mobile and beginning to keep records of property. Thus, the earliest attempts at fixing spoken language in **graphical**, **symbolic** form may have begun with Neolithic counting tokens about nine thousand years ago. As these systems for recording spoken language became more complex, we eventually had something that could indeed fix our narratives, so that we could store them away, making them independent of anyone's individual memory. The creator of the narrative can die and be forgotten – but, if the fixed (written) version of the narrative is preserved, it can be read and replayed hundreds or thousands of years later. There is the inevitable problem that spoken language changes very quickly so that, even if a document still exists, the **code** used to construct it may no longer be in use – a problem that any student who has struggled with Shakespeare (or whoever it was who wrote those plays) will recognise.

If you want to make your narrative known to large numbers of people, you have to find a way of giving other people a copy of it. Before writing systems were invented, the only way of doing this was to arrange for someone else to memorise your story. This is subject to the inherent limitations of the human memory that we have outlined above, and because of this the story will undergo changes as it is passed from one member of a society to another. This will also happen through time, as the story is passed down from one generation to the next. Even after the invention of writing, though, literacy was not widespread, so that the transmission of knowledge and cultural values would still take place orally while literacy remained the preserve of the educated few. Even now, many languages and cultures have no writing system. But in the (post-industrial revolution) Western world we are accustomed to the idea that writing is one way of preserving spoken language.

Written language has now, of course, developed into a **variety** in its own right, but there is little doubt that its original purpose was to transcribe and fix spoken language. One example of this is the fragmentary evidence of Old English poetry in written form – a partial preservation of some artefacts from a purely oral tradition of poetic composition and recital. Having no means, at that time, of mass-producing written text, the educated elite of Anglo-Saxon England could only disseminate copies of poems by writing them out manually and distributing them, very slowly, to a very restricted audience. With the growth of literacy over the next five hundred years, written language began to develop its own features and was no longer simply a brass rubbing of spoken language. Now, in the early twenty-first century, written language has many **dialectal** and **discourse** features distinct from spoken language.

Spoken language is natural. Literacy is artificial. This is why opinion varies about how to teach children to read and write in their early years, and it is why the teaching of literacy is the subject of legislation in many countries. You cannot legislate for the acquisition of spoken language: it happens by itself, given normal social, cognitive and physical development in the child. There is no need for any kind of technology to spread the spoken **forms** and texts of a language: this was given a considerable helping hand by the invention of **analogue** recording equipment in 1877, but be assured it had been happening for many thousands of years prior to that, using the natural storage and retrieval capacity of the human brain. However, because *written* texts are artificial, they need technology to disseminate them. In the middle of the fifteenth century, Johann Gutenberg invented a system for doing this, which remained essentially unchanged for five hundred years. Mass production of written texts, stored and distributed on paper, gave the written forms of language a public profile. The mechanism for retrieval is the scanning of the eye over the page and the cognition of the scanned stream of letters as meaningful language. This is an unnatural process that needs to be taught. Fast forward to the 1930s, and we

5

see the first breakthrough in storing text on media other than paper. The M. Shultz Company's repetitive typewriter used a system of punched cards which operated the keys of the typewriter automatically – in much the same way as a pianola plays a piece of music. Herein was the beginning of document templates being stored for repeated production – the birth of **word processing**. The first machine to be marketed using the term 'word processing' was IBM's Magnetic Tape/Selectric Typewriter or MT/ST in 1964. This used analogue tape as the first reusable medium for storing text – to be replaced by magnetic cards in 1969. In the early 1970s, word-processing machines began to incorporate basic video screens for manipulating text prior to printing, and floppy disk drives for storing text.

Sidestepping a little, and rewinding to 1822, Charles Babbage invented a machine for performing mathematical calculations. Although this machine was destined not to be manufactured until 1991 (when the Science Museum in London followed Babbage's plans to prove that it could be done), the history of computing followed a mechanical path until 1935, when Konrad Zuse began work on an electronic version of his own mechanical calculating machine. Precisely who invented the first **digital** computer remains a matter of debate, but the concept of 'digital switching' to accomplish calculations was famously deployed during the Second World War to break the German Enigma Code, using a computer called Colossus Mark I. These early computers were powered by 'relays' or electrically operated mechanical switches. It was while one such machine was stopped for repair that someone noticed a dead moth in one of the relays (the possible cause of the problem), and this has led to the all too familiar metaphorical term '**bug**' in modern computer troubleshooting. In 1947, work was completed on the **transistor** – a type of **electronic** switch – and this paved the way for the electronics of the personal computer that we are familiar with today. And in 1961, integrated circuits appeared, effectively highly miniaturised transistor circuits, which developed into the microprocessor chips that form the basis of personal computers today.

Getting really wired: the physical context of websites

The Introduction provided the historical and technical background needed to begin to explore the immediate context of websites. We will look at that context in more detail in this unit, and we will begin to explore ways of using that contextual awareness to apply analytical frameworks to websites in a meaningful way.

A TERRIBLE BEAUTY IS BORN: HOW PERSONAL COMPUTERS BEGAN

The first personal computer was marketed by Apple in 1977. Dedicated word-processing machines continued to exist (and do to this day), but if you wanted more power to manipulate text, and also more electronic space to store your documents, you could load some word-processing software into your personal computer. **Software** is simply a set of instructions for the computer, prepared by a computer **programmer**, so that a non-specialist user can 'load' it into the computer. Loading different software can give you many other functions like a searchable 'filing cabinet', a bookkeeping ledger or an arcade game. A dedicated word-processing machine has its software **hard-wired** so that if you want to upgrade to more powerful functions you have to replace the machine. Personal computers marked the separation of machines from software, so that you could keep your old machine but buy new software for it.

A problem for early developers of the personal computer was how to make the user feel that they were working in a familiar environment. To cut a rather complex and technical story very short, the solution to this was the now famous **desktop** metaphor – a working environment that makes the computer **environment** *look like* a desk with a set of filing cabinet draws built into it. To enable the user to control the desk and the filing cabinet, the architects of the personal computer borrowed the **QWERTY keyboard** from the familiar office typewriter, and added a virtual hand that the user could use to delve into the electronic world of the computer and move things around – what we now know as a mouse. Both the desktop and the mouse were invented by Xerox at their Palo Alto Research Center in the 1970s. They still form the basis of the software environment we now know as the **operating system**.

We will always need metaphors to interact with computers. Computers only understand sequences of 1 and 0 (digits or digital information), telling them to open or close millions of tiny switches, but no person can calculate quickly enough to enter the raw numbers (modern computers are too fast and too complicated), so we need a fake world where intuitive manual actions are fed to the computer as raw numbers. This is what software does: it is called the 'operating system' or user interface.

The eternal problem is how to make the computer anticipate how humans think and behave, and how to make people think and behave in a way that the computer can anticipate – a concept that Brenda Laurel (Bardini 1997) has referred to as 'horrible recursion', and one that lies at the heart of user interface design. Not surprisingly, many science fiction writers have imagined that this will conclude with the metaphor becoming a reality – where the computers become so complex that they are capable of changing the conditions of the interface themselves: they become 'conscious'.

EVERYTHING WITHIN: THE ORIGINS OF THE WEB

Web pages are just another software environment, another refinement of the user interface – albeit an influential one, which is why most aspects of the desktop environment on modern personal computers can be made to behave like a web page. But where did web pages come from?

If you want to retrieve a document from a filing cabinet drawer in your own desk, you do not have to leave your seat. If you want to retrieve a document from someone else's desk drawer, you have to get out of your seat and walk or wait for someone to post it to you. Exactly the same was true of the personal computer in the late 1970s and early 1980s. Documents could be made digital and then stored or retrieved from a magnetic disk in their original form – free from error or deterioration. You could even alter the document and store it in a revised form alongside of or instead of the old one. It seemed that printing and writing had come of age and we had finally and completely overcome the error-prone storage and retrieval system of the human brain.

We wanted more though. By the late 1980s, **networking** of large **mainframe** computers (**Wide Area Networks**) had been a reality for many years. Early incarnations of the **Internet** consisted of linked computers that could exchange **packets** of information over long distances – mainly between universities in the United States. This same principle was implemented in the late 1980s for linking personal computers in a business environment – the concept of the **Local Area Network**. It arose from the desire to move and copy documents or **files** from one personal computer to another in an office, thus saving time and money, but it left in place the pathways that, by the mid-1990s, would make possible the information explosion known as the World Wide Web.

Tim Berners-Lee, a physicist frustrated by the fact that his many computing projects at the European Laboratory for Particle Physics were stored on different machines, decided to develop a system that would link these projects together and allow information (or **data**) to travel between them. He wanted it to be a system that would allow a group of physicists to collaborate on several projects simultaneously, without having to move backwards and forwards between several different machines and switch between several different, incompatible, computer environments. He based his new system on **hypertext**, a concept that was influential in the design of computer environments long before the Web. Hypertext stems largely from the ideas of Ted Nelson and Douglas Engelbart.

In the fifteenth century, Gutenberg achieved the mass production of paper documents and books. However, paper documents and books can only be linked physically by placing them in the same physical location. Additionally, the human brain does not naturally concentrate for the entire length of most documents: you have to train yourself to read to the end, and as you read you will think about and see references to other documents that may be about the same topic or connected in other less obvious ways. The brain works by association and connection, and not in the linear way that the post-Gutenberg tradition of literacy requires of the reader.

Hypertext is a way of hard-wiring these associations and connections with other documents – making permanent jumping-off points part of an electronic text, and, if you are linked on a network, the documents can be on other computers twenty feet away – or five thousand miles away. The hard-wired jumping-off points that take you to other documents are called **hyperlinks**. Written text allows us to replay the *content* of our experience and thought, but the revolutionary assumption behind hypertext is that we are replaying a narrative more like the *thought process* itself.

Activity

Text 1: The Electronic Telegraph is a page from http://www.telegraph.co.uk, the website for the *Daily Telegraph* and the *Sunday Telegraph*. The *Daily Telegraph* and the *Sunday Telegraph* were the first national newspapers in the UK to have a **web presence** – launched initially as 'The Electronic Telegraph' in November 1994, fifteen months after the release of the free versions of the **browser** 'Mosaic' for the Microsoft Windows and **Macintosh** operating systems. Given that the release of this software can be seen as the beginning of the World Wide Web as a global **medium**, telegraph.co.uk is an important early pioneer in exploiting the power of the Web. Many of its archived pages are preserved on the site in their original form, so they provide a useful insight into early web page design, using techniques still used today for more basic websites.

1   Remembering that the page is from the web version of a broadsheet newspaper, what immediately strikes you about the appearance of the page, compared with the way you would expect the article to look in print? Here, you could look, for example, at features of **graphology** and layout.

2   Is there a graphological convention for indicating hyperlinks?

3   Can you find any grammatical patterns typical of broadsheet news reporting? Are the patterns you might expect to find in the print version *exactly* the same as in the web version?

4   Comment on how **lexical cohesion** in the page relates to discourse structure. How do these issues relate to narrative, and are we seeing the beginnings of a style and a **reader stance** peculiar to web documents?

5   What do you think is different about the **context of reception** when reading a web article, as opposed to reading a printed article? How does the difference of context relate to any linguistic features you have discovered in the two pages?

Text 1: The Electronic Telegraph

UK News   Electronic Telegraph
Wednesday June 5 1996   Issue 399

Eight arrested in drive to stop soccer thugs
By Ben Fenton

• Grinning suspect sees wake-up call as a compliment

POLICE in London and Manchester yesterday arrested eight men suspected of involvement in football hooliganism in dawn operations designed to deter those intent on causing trouble at the Euro 96 tournament.

The operations also cast doubt on the efficacy of the ticketing system after one of the men was found to have 12 tickets he obtained in his own name.

Four Tottenham Hotspur supporters and two Arsenal fans were arrested in the raids, which started at 5am, at a series of houses across north London and Essex. A seventh man walked into Highgate police station later in the day and was arrested.

Greater Manchester police arrested one man after they visited eight homes in an operation against suspected hooligans. In a separate operation, Manchester officers investigating the activities of the far-Right group Combat 18 arrested three men and seized documents and videos.

In London, Operation Take-Off, involving more than 70 officers and four dog-handlers, recovered the Euro 96 tickets, a sword, a bayonet and three knives.

Five adults and a juvenile were charged last night with violent disorder.

Police moved after studying video film of a fight at the Arsenal-Spurs game at Highbury in April which involved 30 to 40 hooligans attempting to reach each other through a thinly-defended cordon of police officers and stewards.

Seats and punches were thrown and a policeman was knocked unconscious. It seems that by inviting the media to witness the raids, the Metropolitan Police was keen to make clear its intentions with the European Championship due to start on Saturday.

The man arrested yesterday had four tickets for England's opening game with Switzerland and four for the following weekend's clash with Scotland

Det Chief Insp Dave Crompton, who led the raid, said police intelligence showed that those arrested were planning on going to Euro 96, and added: "Today we have sent out a message for the tournament and for next season as well - just be aware that if you are intending to cause trouble, we will identify you and we will arrest you."

He also issued a set of six photos of other Arsenal and Tottenham supporters still wanted for questioning and asked for help from the public in identifying them.

The recovery of tickets obtained legitimately by a man suspected by police of being a football troublemaker will be seen as worrying by the FA, which is responsible for selling seats for the tournament.

The man arrested yesterday had four tickets for England's opening game with Switzerland and four for the following weekend's clash with Scotland. Two other tickets were recovered and another two, which he had also apparently obtained legitimately, were not found in the search.

An extensive computer system has been established by the organisers designed to prevent known hooligans getting tickets for any matches.

Northumbria police raided a number of homes last week and published more than 100 pictures of suspects following an outbreak of football-related violence in Newcastle on the last day of the season last month.

Police who arrested three men at a house in Oldham, Greater Manchester, yesterday said it was the culmination of a three-month investigation into Combat 18. A spokesman said: "It is understood the men arrested have international connections and their involvement at Euro 96 cannot be discounted."

• A police dog called Benson recovered Scotland's Euro 96 football kit two hours after it had been stolen from Ettington Park Hotel in Alderminster, near Stratford, Warwicks, on Monday.

The thieves, who have not been caught, snatched 20 to 30 bags of kit, each worth £500, minutes after a delivery van from the manufacturer had drawn up outside the hotel, the Scottish team's base for their matches at Villa Park, Birmingham. The bags were found hidden in nearby woodland.

4 June 1996: England players close ranks over jet damage

Next Story: In Chicago, the Princess practises her new role

Reply to **Electronic Telegraph**

Electronic Telegraph is a Registered Service Mark of The Telegraph plc

Because the Web was initially conceived as a medium for handling information, its original specification did not contain a huge number of possibilities for sophisticated layout. It was not much more than **rich text** with the ability to turn selected portions of text into hyperlinks. It was possible to include images and to make these into hyperlinks, but because of the relatively slow **download** speeds of **modems** in the mid-1990s, web developers had to be careful about images. It was common for browsers to be **configured** only to load the text from a web page.

So, compared with some of the familiar layout conventions of broadsheet newspapers, this page might at first appear unsophisticated. It is not laid out in columns, and it makes use of only one **typeface** in three sizes – one for the **body text**, sub-headings and byline, one for the headline, and one for the **date line** and issue number. Professional publishing traditionally uses two varieties of typeface or **font**: **serif** fonts, such as Times New Roman (characterised by tapered flourishes at the ends of letter strokes) and **sans serif** fonts (having no flourishes) such as Arial. (The word 'font' more properly means the specific point size and style of typeface, for example, 'Times New Roman 14 point bold', but it is fair to say that usage is now blurring the semantic distinction between 'typeface' and 'font'.) For several centuries, printing was dominated by serif typefaces, but the addition of sans serif typefaces in the nineteenth century eventually led to professional typographers having a choice of the two main typeface styles. Sans serif tends to be used for headlines, or to give a contemporary feel to the text.

Why, then, do we not see any sans serif typefaces in use in Text 1? The answer lies in the development of word processing. Computer-based word processing took the home and small business user into the realms of professional publishing and gave them access to **proportionally spaced** typefaces, as used in printed books and newspapers, liberating them from the artificial **monospaced** typefaces such as Courier which were only developed to fit in with the mechanical limitations of the typewriter. (Monospaced typefaces are now really only used to give a 'retro' feel to documents – the pragmatic message that the text is somehow functional and has been produced on a budget.) For these reasons, all word-processing software defaults to a serif font at a size of around 12 point, seen as a de facto standard for print publishing and business communication. The same was, and is, true of software tools used to create web pages. If you do not tell the browser to display using a different font, it will default to something very like Times New Roman 12 point. So, the fact that a national newspaper chose to publish web pages using typographical defaults, without striving to create a visual **house style**, suggests that in 1996 there were technological constraints that prevented them from doing so.

It is also noticeable that the paragraphs are **blocked** rather than **indented**. This has become standard practice in web publishing and differs from current practice in newspaper publishing. It originates from the fact that paragraph indentation was either impossible or very cumbersome in the original implementation of **HTML**, the technical language used to code web pages. (See Unit six, pp. 87–94, for a more detailed discussion of HTML.)

Despite these constraints, it is interesting to note that the page preserves the main traditional elements of newspaper layout, including the **masthead**.

What of the reading experience though? Returning to our discussion above about the retrieval and playback of narratives, are we seeing here the birth of a fundamentally different way of reading? In print publishing, underlining is a relatively rare technique, having only been included in word processors because people had become accustomed to it on typewriters, but blue underlined text quickly became the standard for indicating hyperlinks in web publishing. It is also customary for the colour of the text to change when the hyperlink has been used, so already we have a dynamic interactivity quite alien to the medium of print.

In order to read the stories referred to by the hyperlinks, it is very tempting to click on the link *before* you have finished reading the article. Then, when you are reading the next article you are offered several more links. From this point of view, it is very difficult to test web documents against traditional narrative models.

One of the most influential of these models has been the one put forward by **Tzvetan Todorov** (1981) which is based primarily on the idea of equilibrium or balance. The narrative begins with a kind of equilibrium, and then a problem, or **enigma,** arises which the rest of the narrative is designed to solve. The engine of the narrative thus makes us want to continue reading until the equilibrium is restored. Todorov was keen to emphasise that it was not the *same* equilibrium that was restored, and that there was always some kind of transformation involved in the unfolding of the story.

Now, while this model applies in various very satisfying ways to film and literary narrative, and can also be applied very effectively to non-fictional discourses such as newspaper articles and documentaries, we have a problem with hypertext because in a real sense the narrative is never finished, and there are more ways of navigating the available paths than a reader can pursue in a lifetime.

Traditional narratives are basically **linear**: there may be more than one line of development (as in the various storylines of a soap opera) but the plots follow a line and are heading (eventually) for some kind of conclusion. In contrast, a better way of imagining hypertext discourse would be to think of it resembling one of those spider diagrams that we have all been taught to use for planning essays. A page can be connected to maybe ten other pages, using hyperlinks, and then each of those ten pages can be connected to ten others, either on the same site or another site maybe thousands of miles away (distance is not important on the Web). It is similar to navigating with road signs but without a map: you choose your route, and if you are not thinking about where you are going you may have trouble finding your way back. In hypertext theory the 'towns' you encounter on the way, where you have a choice of several different roads to other destinations, are called **nodes**. Another useful metaphor to bear in mind, when thinking about discourse and narrative in relation to websites, is that the experience is very akin to a TV viewer 'channel hopping'.

In terms of grammatical and lexical patterns, a lot of Text 1 can be analysed in the same way as a printed newspaper article, as much of the text is a transcript of the printed edition of the newspaper. For example, the use of **dynamic verbs** and the omission of determiners in newspaper headlines are both standard features of linguistic newspaper analysis; there would also be a lot of mileage in looking at **verb tenses**. However, we begin to see *new* linguistic patterns associated with web language when we look at the grammatical units that have been isolated as hyperlinks. It is common to use a noun phrase as a hyperlink, a convention that comes from titling in print media, but here we see examples of **verb phrases**, often with subjects and **objects**, being made into hyperlinks. In the case of 'we will identify you and we will arrest you', we can see a similarity with the use of **pull quotes** as sub-headings in tabloid newspaper reporting, but, as a general trend, the use of verb phrases as lexical gateways to other documents is a convention that has been developed and defined by the use of hypertext and the Web.

THE MARCH OF TIME: DEVELOPMENTS IN WEB DESIGN

There is much more to say about how early web documents were setting standards for a relationship with the viewer/reader that was fundamentally different from the print relationship, but the ideas discussed in the activity above should give you some fertile ground for considering your own investigations into web discourse. We will close this unit by bringing the picture up to date and looking at the development of some key linguistic features in web page construction in the time since Text 1 was produced.

Activity

Text 2: telegraph.co.uk is another article from http://www.telegraph.co.uk published much more recently. It deals with a similar topic, but as you will see, even from just a cursory glance, its presentation is much more sophisticated.

1   At time of writing, the URL of Text 2 is http://www.telegraph. co.uk/news/main.jhtml?xml=%2Fnews%2F2003%2F04%2F04%2 Fnhool04.xml. If you have access to Internet, go to the page and examine which parts of the page are hyperlinks. How does the design of the hyperlinks differ from the earlier page?

2   Is there a wider variety of lexical content being offered to you on this page? If so, why do you think this is?

3   Does this page seem to indicate a change in the *nature* of the Web since Text 1 was produced? In other words, do websites have a different, more complex purpose now? Explain your answer.

Text 2: telegraph.co.uk

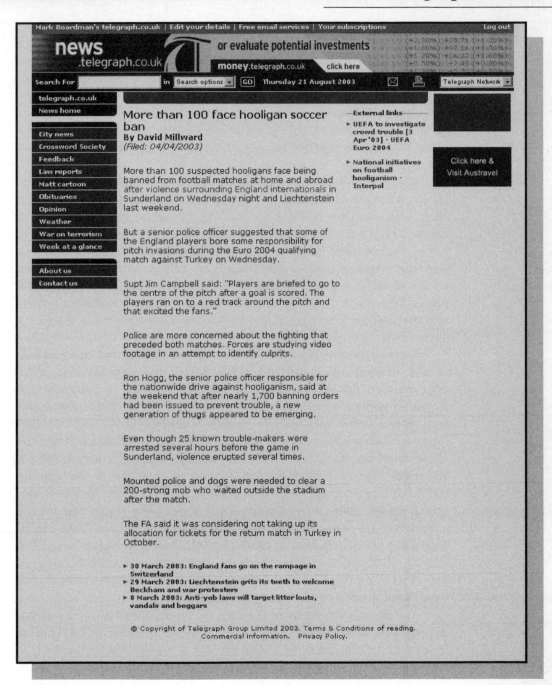

Mark Boardman's telegraph.co.uk | Edit your details | Free email services | Your subscriptions   Log out

news
.telegraph.co.uk   or evaluate potential investments

money.telegraph.co.uk   click here

Search For [   ] in [Search options ▼] [GO] Thursday 21 August 2003

Telegraph Network ▼

telegraph.co.uk
News home

City news
Crossword Society
Feedback
Law reports
Matt cartoon
Obituaries
Opinion
Weather
War on terrorism
Week at a glance

About us
Contact us

More than 100 face hooligan soccer ban
By David Millward
(Filed: 04/04/2003)

More than 100 suspected hooligans face being banned from football matches at home and abroad after violence surrounding England internationals in Sunderland on Wednesday night and Liechtenstein last weekend.

But a senior police officer suggested that some of the England players bore some responsibility for pitch invasions during the Euro 2004 qualifying match against Turkey on Wednesday.

Supt Jim Campbell said: "Players are briefed to go to the centre of the pitch after a goal is scored. The players ran on to a red track around the pitch and that excited the fans."

Police are more concerned about the fighting that preceded both matches. Forces are studying video footage in an attempt to identify culprits.

Ron Hogg, the senior police officer responsible for the nationwide drive against hooliganism, said at the weekend that after nearly 1,700 banning orders had been issued to prevent trouble, a new generation of thugs appeared to be emerging.

Even though 25 known trouble-makers were arrested several hours before the game in Sunderland, violence erupted several times.

Mounted police and dogs were needed to clear a 200-strong mob who waited outside the stadium after the match.

The FA said it was considering not taking up its allocation for tickets for the return match in Turkey in October.

▸ **30 March 2003: England fans go on the rampage in Switzerland**
▸ **29 March 2003: Liechtenstein grits its teeth to welcome Beckham and war protesters**
▸ **8 March 2003: Anti-yob laws will target litter louts, vandals and beggars**

External links
▸ UEFA to investigate crowd trouble [3 Apr '03] - UEFA Euro 2004

▸ National initiatives on football hooliganism - Interpol

Click here & Visit Austravel

Commentary

The Web has developed from a medium of information exchange and archiving in the academic community, to the most commercially significant global medium to emerge in the latter part of the twentieth century, and this new competitive agenda is very clearly reflected in the page design of Text 2. Use of graphical elements is now mandatory in web page design, and each web designer will use blocks of colour in a way individual to that particular site, trying to achieve consistency across the site and establish a house style. In this case, the house style is crucial in **branding** the company that has created it.

Much of this is driven by fashions in web page design, and one current fashion is the use of **sidebars** to highlight and formalise possible navigation choices to other parts of the site, combined with **white space** to divide and categorise the types of navigation available. An aspect of this categorisation is the 'About us' and 'Contact us' sidebar, separated from the hyperlinks to the other main sections of the newspaper. This has become a standard feature of many institutional websites, repeated as a **motif** on most of the pages. It carries two main pragmatic messages: that the website's owner-ship and identity is unequivocal, and that the organisation can always be approached.

The masthead (top left) has developed from simple text into a sophis-ticated graphical logo, significantly different from the masthead used on the print version of the newspaper. Interesting features of the masthead include a cropped portion of the masthead from the print version of the newspaper, reinforcing the link with the print edition and emphasising that although this is an **online** edition, it still takes its authenticity and history from the long-established reputation of the *Daily Telegraph* and the *Sunday Telegraph*. The word 'news' is part of the URL for the news section of the website, but it has been isolated, lifted and given a larger font size so that it also acts as a title. Significantly, though, it still is not given upper case for the initial letter – a very pervasive typographical feature that has taken hold, largely due to the influence of email and **SMS text messaging** (where the absence of upper case comes from the subconscious contextual assump-tion that the messages need to be sent quickly, and that the monitoring of typographical patterns militates against this).

The panel immediately to the right of the masthead is called a **rotat-ing banner advertisement**. These advertisements are timed to be replaced by another advertisement, or a different part of the same advertisement, at intervals of a few seconds, as you will see if you load the page yourself. Very often (as here) banners are linked together with a simple narrative. The graphical background is suggestive of business and accountancy, while the text presents portions of a sentence at short enough intervals for most people to remember the portion that came before. The isolated **clause** 'evaluate potential investments' introduced by the **coordinating conjunction** 'or' is not syntactically possible, so even if it is the first banner to appear, when you visit the page, you know to expect contextualisation from the appearance of the next banner or maybe the one after next. Banners set up an expectation of a **cyclic narrative**, and readers are accustomed to beginning their reading of the cycle from any randomly generated point.

Thinking back to Text 1, it is immediately noticeable that the practice of using the default serif typeface has been abandoned. All of the text on the page appears in sans serif typeface – a practice that is currently very widespread on institutional websites. (For a more detailed discussion of the reasons behind this, see Units two and five, pp. 21–36 and 67–86.) It is also interesting that paragraph blocking is still in use, even though changes in HTML since 1996 have meant that indented paragraphs are now easy to implement on web pages. This indicates that web publishing has now developed graphological conventions of its own, distinct from the medium of print. Also, we still have a white background. Although the use of graphical backgrounds became a common feature in amateur web publishing, and remains so, the professional trend is still to use either white or another uniform colour. One of the main reasons for this is that it is very difficult to find a graphical background that does not interfere with the reading of the text on the page.

The graphology of the hyperlink is now liberated from the default underlined version. Any area of the page, text or graphics, is potentially a hyperlink, and an accepted component of the reader's stance in relation to web pages is now the assumption that the reader has to actively look for hyperlinks: moving the mouse around the page and waiting for the mouse cursor to change into a graphical pointing finger, is as routine a part of the reading process as turning the pages in a book.

Elements of interactivity beyond the hyperlink have become standard in the vast majority of websites. One key development here has been the emergence of **streaming media** – a feature that will be explored in Unit four (see pp. 53–65) – but in Text 2 we have examples of two more common interactive features: drop-down menus and **database** searching. The growth in complexity and size of websites since the mid-1990s has meant that it is now sometimes necessary to bypass hyperlink browsing in order to find information within a realistic time frame. Hence the fact that a **search dialogue** tends to be a repeated motif, **foregrounded** by its placing near the top of the page.

SUMMARY

In this opening unit we have looked at the historical context of the development of websites in relation to the development of the technology that made them possible. The picture emerges of a mass medium that grew almost by accident, within the space of three or four years, and is now at least as influential as television in affecting the marketing decisions of commercial and non-commercial organisations. We have also begun to explore how the established tools of linguistic analysis can be adapted to shed light on some of the stylistic patterns of websites. The Web is still largely a medium that relies on written language to carry its meaning, but other elements of site content have become increasingly important – and, while it is crucial to realise that there would be no World Wide Web without the existence of print, we now need to liberate ourselves from that legacy and develop analytical concepts that are uniquely applicable to websites.

Extension

1   Track the development of a specific news story in the print and web editions of the same newspaper. How much evidence is there of a different **sub-editing** process for web-based news?

2   From a linguistic perspective, compare the house styles of different web-based newspapers. Is there a trend in the design of pages for Internet news publishing that differs from patterns you can see in other categories of website (for example, websites for book publishing companies)?

3   Conduct a survey of how many people in your age group have access to **broadband** Internet at home. Try to build in some analysis of whether this factor affects the kind of website that they habitually visit. Does the fact that you access the Internet via a **dial-up** modem affect your attitude to websites in general? Is the growth of broadband access to the Internet changing the balance of written and spoken language on websites, and how useful are the traditional tools of textual analysis in the light of this?

Front-of-house: institutional websites

Having tried out some analytical frameworks on a couple of web pages in their technological context in Unit one, we now need to turn our attention to specific types of website, and look at whether different types of website need different analytical frameworks or more specific contextual knowledge in order to read them effectively.

VIRTUALLY THERE: WEBSITES AS METAPHORICAL BUILDINGS

The Web is now so well developed as a mainstream mass communication medium that most organisations are considered foolish if they do not have a presence on it. Until quite recently, if you wanted to see a company or a university doing its daily work, you would have to go there and walk through the main entrance to the reception desk. Now, it is possible to get a broadly similar experience by just guessing the web address of the company or university and typing it into the address bar of Internet Explorer. For example, put in 'http://www.microsoft. com', hit enter, and you will find the correct site: the Internet pretty much knows where you want to go today.

Of course, organisations have always published flyers, leaflets and magazines to guide the public on the ins and outs of the work they do and the services they offer – and partly from this has come the commonly held idea that web pages are really just fancy versions of printed text: print media have supposedly come of age technologically. The truth, however, is a little bit more 'out there'. It is often more helpful to see the high-budget web presence of a major organisation as something resembling a building with multiple offices, conference suites, corridors, lifts and all manner of areas where information is stored. How those different parts of the building signal to you that they are available to look at, and in some cases get things from, is all to do with how the front part of the site is designed – if you will, the entrance and reception area of the building. In this unit we will take a look at the linguistic side of these signalling devices.

Activity

A viewer/reader of Text 3: Salford University could be anyone in any circumstances:

◎   casual 'surfers'

◎   potential UCAS applicants

◎   university employees

◎   university inspectors.

All these people could be connecting from anywhere in the world at any time of day – and they could have been online for five minutes or four hours. The site could be exactly what they were looking for, and they could be intent on staying there, or the audience could equally consist of people who are killing time while an mp3 or video file downloads in the background; many of them will have found their way to the site via a search engine. Examine the different linguistic ways in which Text 3 tries to set up a relationship with the viewer/reader and keep them at that particular site.

Text 3: Salford University

The University of Salford
www.salford.ac.uk

A GREATER MANCHESTER *UNIVERSITY*

General information
About the University
Faculties and Schools
Research
Postgraduate Study
Publications
Maps and Access Routes
Contacts

Business
Services to Business and the
Community

GET ON
CLICK HERE

Applicants
Choose Salford
Course Information
How to Apply
Information for prospective students
Information for schools & colleges
Accommodation
Courses for Clearing 2003

Staff / Students / Alumni
Intranet
Information for Students
Library and Computing
Education Liaison
International Office
Alumni
Message Boards
Student Payment Centre
Personnel Division
Policies and Procedures
Links

Can't find something ?
Online Reception
A-Z Site Index
Search

News and Events
Latest news:
Record breaking success for Salford adventurer
Shock Radio 97.6M
Train to interpret for the Police and Court Services in England and Wales
Important announcements
New Courses for September/October 2003
Calling Current International Students: Visa renewals
The BA Festival of Science
Open Days
Visit Salford University before applying
Research Assessment Exercise 2001 - the results
Forthcoming events
01/09/2003 Second International Conference on Biomechanics of the Lower Limb in Health Disease and Rehabilitiation
01/09/2003 Paul Needham
04/09/2003 Understanding Britain
06/09/2003 British Association Festival of Science
09/09/2003 Fire in the Park
13/09/2003 Flying Start for Women into Business
17/09/2003 Education in a Changing Environment - Conference
see all news and events »

UNIVERSITY OF SALFORD, SALFORD, GREATER MANCHESTER M5 4WT, UK. TELEPHONE +44 (0)161 295 5000
Choose Salford | Course information | Research and postgraduate study
Services to business and the community | Applying to Salford | News and events | Travel information | Contacts | Webmaster
If you can't find what you're looking for please visit our online reception or search the site
All information copyright University of Salford 2003

Search

THE QUEEN'S
ANNIVERSARY PRIZES
2000

Commentary

The first noticeable graphological feature is the use of a sans serif font in the majority of the text. Everything that is not part of a logo or masthead appears in a sans serif font. Fonts are closely linked to **register** and levels of formality, and the use of a sans serif font in the body text is a sign that the institution wants to appear contemporary and modern: pragmatic meaning is embodied graphologically. Serif fonts are reserved for areas of the text that need to signal permanence and tradition – for example, the name of the university in the logo at the top of the page. For example, Salford is a university likely to pride itself on maintaining courses that are relevant to modern society, but at the same time it would want to encapsulate the idea that it has the same academic strength and reliability as some of the older universities.

Syntax is also linked to different language registers. Graphologically, the page designer has gone for a minimalist feel with lots of uniform, open space; which can in turn be linked to patterns of syntactic minimalism. There are very few complete sentences on the page, of which the following is the most grammatically complex: 'If you can't find what you're looking for please visit our online reception or search the site.' Significantly, it is presented in a much smaller font size than the rest of the text, and placed at the bottom of the page – it is a sentence containing conditionally dependent clauses offering the user an alternative strategy if the main default page does not immediately fulfil their needs.

The main part of the page contains only visually discrete, linguistically easily processed syntactic units, most of which are not complete sentences. They fall into two main groups: simple noun phrases and **post-modified** noun phrases. Some of the simpler noun phrases are to be found at the top of each main list, inside a bar – a graphological way of signalling broad semantic categories that a visitor to the site might be interested in, or of anticipating the social group that the visitor might identify with. Many of the hyperlinks offered under each of the headings can be seen to correspond with actual physical locations within the university campus – a point that underlines our central metaphor for this unit: that of a default institutional page which functions very much like the reception area of a large building. The 'News and Events' section is the web equivalent of a pinboard where information is regularly rotated – a board that visitors may browse before they decide which part of the building to enter, or before they decide to visit the reception area of another building.

All these elements combine to cater very effectively for multiple audiences and contexts of reception. No matter what your background or reason for visiting the site, you are clear about the university's attitude to the general public – and you do not have to do too much reading to get this message. Of course, the reception metaphor does not stretch all the way: if people visited real institutional buildings in this kind of casual way, without indicating their presence there, it would create serious security issues. But perhaps this in itself raises a further point: that it is the user who has the power on the Web. Companies and organisations feel obligated to have a presence there, but they are fighting for a profile in a world that is essentially **unregulated** and has a life of its own.

One further extrapolation of the noticeboard metaphor comes from how the virtual foyer of the building responds to changing events. The hyperlink 'Courses for Clearing 2003' and the black circle which alternates the text

'GET ON' with 'GET IN', superimposed with a graphical button that acts as a hyperlink displaying the text 'CLICK HERE', are all page elements added *after* the publication of A Level and VCE results. Imperative, dynamic verbs 'get' and 'click' pragmatically reflect and imply urgency, linked to the anticipated context of having your results but being without a place. Returning to our metaphor, this could be likened to the setting-up of a special exhibition or information desk in the foyer of the building.

You will be familiar from Unit one with the visual convention of underlining hyperlinks on a web page, and making them appear in blue text. Nowadays there are **hover buttons** and many other visually striking ways of handling hyperlinks, but most sites have never really abandoned the old convention of blue underlined text. As you will see if you visit the page at http://www.salford.ac.uk, the Salford site uses a clever inversion of this old web convention, by making the hyperlinks into hover buttons which only become underlined when the mouse cursor is over them, thus indicating contemporary relevance as well as paying homage to the beginnings of a tradition in web design.

The arrangement and wording of the hyperlinks on a front-of-house institutional website is very important for the instant map it generates of where you can go from this virtual reception area. The way the hyperlinks are presented can make the difference between a viewer/reader following one of the links or hitting the Back button on the browser toolbar. If you've based the root of your search using a search engine, then the Back button is your return path to your list of **hits**; but if you find a link that intrigues you, the hyper-narrative moves forward and you enter the site – even if that decision is only motivated by the fact that your mp3 or *Simpsons* episode has not quite downloaded yet, or the kettle has not quite boiled. All web designers are aware of this hyper-narrative phenomenon, and they must exploit it if their site is to be commercially viable.

The pragmatic force of a logo is always to give some kind of validity to the organisation. In a purely commercial context, it is usually about corporate identity and recognition. In the case of Text 2, the logo at the bottom of the page is more to do with *other* organisations reinforcing the validity of the university. This particular logo is not a hyperlink, but many such logos appearing on institutional pages *are*, in case you want to pursue (as a narrative possibility) exactly how this extra validity is being offered.

Referring again to Text 2, the image at the top of the page is deliberately small and representational in one or two interesting ways: the implication is that Salford University combines aesthetically pleasing elements of urban life and tradition, but also promises aspects of a more pastoral environment. Often, the picture on this part of a site changes on a regular basis, almost in the same way as a company or educational institution might change the artwork on display in its foyer, in order to avoid letting its image become stale.

The linguistic point here is that this message is being conveyed *without* language. You will often find that, in decoding complex transactional texts such as websites, what is left out is as important as what is included. Multiple contexts are hard to anticipate using language, and so very often the web designer will go for a visual **semiology** instead of a linguistic one.

BASIC BURGER – NOTHING ON IT: DEVELOPMENTS IN WEB GRAPHICS

A further discussion point under the heading of pragmatics and narrative comes from the absence on the Salford site of the simple noun phrase 'text-only version', which is now a relatively rare find on any kind of website but, until very recently, could be found on some university websites. It was there so that we could make the narrative decision to *reject* the site in its default form and opt for a version more suited to older technology: pages with a high graphical content will load very slowly with connections using modems manufactured before about 1999, so a version without graphics (similar to Text 1 in Unit one) was routinely made available.

This kind of technological democracy is now more or less defunct in a developed world driven by ever cheaper computer hardware, faster Internet connections (the move away from modems to broadband), and more easily available software, so that many high-end commercial sites have a baseline **system requirement** (**hardware** and software). Some sites will even perform an automatic check of your system, offering to install appropriate software **plug-ins** for you so that the site will work properly.

To return to the significance of 'text-only version', though, it was about a **subtext** saying that they are a technologically democratic institution that does not withhold information on the grounds of hardware specification – which is why university websites were some of the last to offer text-only versions. To see one still in use, have a look at http://www.leeds.gov.uk/default.asp?style=&view=text where the fact that it is a text-only version is very clearly foregrounded linguistically (because language is all you have in a world without graphics), and you are offered the narrative choice to return to the more colourful, image-driven twenty-first century Web, or continue in your time warp if you really insist.

Bearing in mind the underlying front-of-house metaphor, look at Text 4: Lake Coghlan, the default page for a company offering ICT development packages and troubleshooting, along with more general marketing advice, to the legal industry and general business community.

1   Are the linguistic patterns here similar to those that we discovered in Text 3?

2   Is there any linguistic evidence that we are dealing with a different type of institution? Are different assumptions being made about target audience?

Text 4: Lake Coghlan

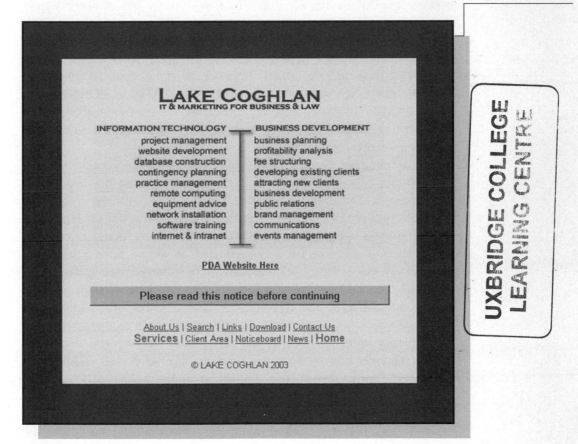

27

Commentary

Again, we have the use of a serif typeface to create the brand image of the organisation, incorporating some interesting modern adaptations of traditional typography. The typeface used for the company name does not have a lower-case character set, but uses smaller versions of upper-case letters instead (i.e. **small caps**). Also, the typeface itself is from a modern sub-category of serif, called **slab serif** (wider strokes and less tapering on the serifs), invented in the nineteenth century to fulfil the need for visually striking typefaces in the context of a growing advertising industry and rising levels of literacy. This subtle updating of established typographical practice then carries a subtext suggesting that the company is contemporary and technologically clued up, at the same time as keeping an eye on tradition and the value of established procedures.

It is common now for web designers to look for innovative ways of handling graphical behaviour when the mouse cursor moves over a hyperlink. In this case, instead of the hyperlink underlining itself, a red triangle is produced, pointing outwards from the central bar to the appropriate heading – imitating the behaviour of business presentational aids such as PowerPoint slides and flip charts. However, at the bottom of the screen there are still some examples of more traditional, text-based hyperlinks – paying homage to earlier web design principles. A subtextual reading of this could be that the designer might want to give a higher profile to the core services offered by the company.

Grammatically, Text 3 is an excellent example of the principle of using noun phrases as **portals** to key areas of the virtual company building. (Some of the phrases – for example, 'attracting new clients' – can be analysed as non-finite verb phrases, but they can be considered functionally equivalent to noun phrases because they could occupy the **subject**, object or **complement** slot in a sentence.) It is notable that *all* of the noun phrases are **abstract** whereas in Text 2 some of them were **concrete** noun phrases used metaphorically, such as 'message board'. This suggests different assumptions about audience and context. The Lake Coghlan site is unlikely to be a haven for casual surfers but, once it has attracted its target audience to the virtual reception area, it will need to be very specific about the services on offer and provide very carefully tailored portals. There is an assumption that lawyers have a high order understanding of formal language, and that they will not need abstract concepts to be embodied using familiar metaphors. They will need to manage time effectively, so if the reception area does not signpost its services unequivocally, the reader will look elsewhere.

One further syntactically interesting point is that there is again only one complete sentence on the page, following the principle that virtual reception areas will tend to avoid complete sentences unless they are needed to formalise some of the conditions of the transaction the reader enters into when viewing the site.

MARKING TERRITORY: WEB ADDRESS NAMES

Many of the sites analysed in this book use an Internet marketing technique called **domain name branding**. This is where the organisation tries to make sure that the address or URL of the site is as similar to the name of the organisation as possible. The reasoning is that most Internet users do not have complex searching skills, and if they can remember the name of an organisation they are very likely to try and reach its web presence by simply typing the name of the company in the address box at the top of the browser; most people have now also been **socialised** into the habit of adding 'www' before the name and trying elements like 'com' or 'co.uk' after the name, with the added proviso that a 'dot' separates elements of a URL.

A little technical background should begin to shed some light on the linguistic significance of domain name branding. As we are already aware, physical distance has no significance on the Web. You can sit in your attic or cellar, and you can load a page **hosted** on a computer (or **server**) located five thousand miles away, with no noticeable delay. The page could also be located on a server at the end of your street, and you may not notice the difference in the time it takes to load. Whenever a page loads into your browser, the server is simply allowing you to receive a copy of the page (or download it). The system that allows these copies to move around the Internet is called **Hypertext Transfer Protocol** (invented by Tim Berners-Lee: see Unit one, pp. 7–20), which is why all web addresses have 'http' in front of them. The browser contacts a special server called a **Domain Name Server (DNS)** and this server tells the browser the physical location of the page so that the browser can retrieve a copy of the page. Basically, the domain is just the name of the computer. The Internet is one massive computer network, and all computers on a network need to have a name that is unique.

In the early days, it was necessary for all computer names (server names) on the Web to begin with 'www', but this is becoming less of a requirement now. After the **domain name**, the server will be looking for the name of the file (document, page) that you want from the server. Names of documents have to come after a forward slash '/' so that the server and browser know the difference between a computer name (or domain) and a **filename**. If no document name is given, the server will send you a default document usually called 'index.html', 'home.html' or 'default.html'.

So, when you type http://www.microsoft.com in your address bar, you are asking ·for the default page on the server with that name. A domain name can only be registered once, to one organisation or one person, so from a corporate branding point of view it could be a disaster if someone else beats you to registering a domain name that contains your company name.

From a linguistic point of view, one of the most noteworthy features of domain names is that only part of the domain contains recognisable **lexemes**. Frequently, it is a noun – the name of a company or individual. The reader sees the 'www' portion as a necessary empty **morpheme**: even if you do not understand why, you still need to include it. A similar attitude exists to elements on the end of the domain name, with the added dimension that there is an increasing number of possibilities as to what these could be. Large organisations will register the '.com' and '.net' versions and usually the country specific version, so that a large UK company will have the '.co.uk' – where the trailing portion of the domain name *is* lexically significant. But there is a confusing array of other possibilities like '.net', '.info', '.edu' and '.biz', all of which lead to a kind of **morpho-lexical** angst whereby you know the name of the organisation but you are not sure which half-understood elements should follow it after the dot – a sense that there is a syntax, but that it eludes you, as if you are trying to communicate in a foreign language.

There is a chance that you will be taken to the right page. But you could equally generate a 'DNS Error' whereby your **Internet Service Provider (ISP)** tells you that the name you have tried does not have a DNS entry; or you could find that the domain name you have tried is registered to an organisation wholly unrelated to the one you had in mind, so that you are taken to a page that is irrelevant or even distasteful. Occasionally, a domain hosting company will tell you that someone has **'parked'** the domain with them but not got around to using it for presenting any content. Part of the frustration that some people feel with the Web as a medium arises from the feeling that their

hyper-narrative can get off to many false starts before it yields anything of value. If a company or organisation has got its domain name branding right, these false starts can be minimised or even eliminated.

MAPPING TERRITORY: FINDING YOUR WAY AROUND

As we suggested in Unit one, hypertext narrative can gain a momentum that seems unstoppable and it certainly appears determined to elude conventional narrative models. Once you begin to click on hyperlinks, you can travel through several nodes and end up on a journey that appears to have no pattern and no possible resolution other than switching off the computer.

When **intertextuality** consists of hard-wired links and not simply references that the readers have to pursue themselves, it is easy to think of the Web as a wilderness. But it is perhaps more appropriate to think of it as a series of interconnected buildings. Some of these buildings are better kept than others, and where the building is very large and contains a large number of rooms and corridors, it is customary for the web designer to provide a **site map**.

Text 5: telegraph.co.uk is the front-of-house page for telegraph.co. uk. Here you can see example of a complex corporate site, where the degree of complexity in the organisation of hypertext-linking mechanisms within the site has been anticipated by the provision of a site map in the reception area. The question arises: why not simply use the map to navigate the site, and bypass the virtual reception area? If you go to http://www.telegraph.co.uk you will be able to click on the site map in the bottom left corner. This will show you a very raw version of the hypertext discourse structure on the site – comprehensive, but based only on text links organised alphabetically. It is a far more pleasurable, visually rewarding experience to go in through the portals offered by the virtual reception area.

All this suggests that the site map is there as a fail-safe in case you do not find what you are looking for. Usable search facilities are a relatively recent development, but they have now become standard on most professionally produced websites and have largely replaced site maps. Site maps are an older tradition, but many designers still provide them.

Text 5: telegraph.co.uk

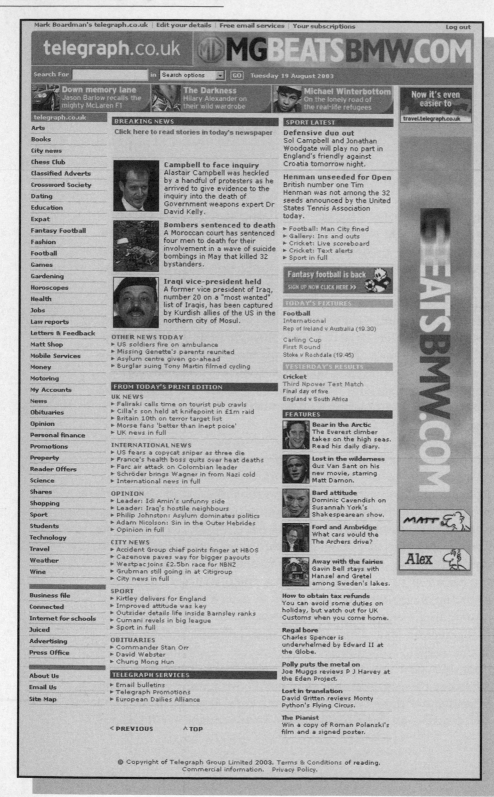

telegraph.co.uk   MG BEATS BMW.COM

Search For [   ] in [Search options ▼] [GO]   Tuesday 19 August 2003

Down memory lane
Jason Barlow recalls the mighty McLaren F1

The Darkness
Hilary Alexander on their wild wardrobe

Michael Winterbottom
On the lonely road of the real-life refugees

Now it's even easier to

travel.telegraph.co.uk

telegraph.co.uk

- Arts
- Books
- City news
- Chess Club
- Classified Adverts
- Crossword Society
- Dating
- Education
- Expat
- Fantasy Football
- Fashion
- Football
- Games
- Gardening
- Horoscopes
- Health
- Jobs
- Law reports
- Letters & Feedback
- Matt Shop
- Mobile Services
- Money
- Motoring
- My Accounts
- News
- Obituaries
- Opinion
- Personal finance
- Promotions
- Property
- Reader Offers
- Science
- Shares
- Shopping
- Sport
- Students
- Technology
- Travel
- Weather
- Wine

- Business file
- Connected
- Internet for schools
- Juiced
- Advertising
- Press Office

- About Us
- Email Us
- Site Map

BREAKING NEWS

Click here to read stories in today's newspaper

Campbell to face inquiry
Alastair Campbell was heckled by a handful of protesters as he arrived to give evidence to the inquiry into the death of Government weapons expert Dr David Kelly.

Bombers sentenced to death
A Moroccan court has sentenced four men to death for their involvement in a wave of suicide bombings in May that killed 32 bystanders.

Iraqi vice-president held
A former vice president of Iraq, number 20 on a "most wanted" list of Iraqis, has been captured by Kurdish allies of the US in the northern city of Mosul.

OTHER NEWS TODAY
- US soldiers fire on ambulance
- Missing Genette's parents reunited
- Asylum centre given go-ahead
- Burglar suing Tony Martin filmed cycling

FROM TODAY'S PRINT EDITION

UK NEWS
- Faliraki calls time on tourist pub crawls
- Cilla's son held at knifepoint in £1m raid
- Britain 10th on terror target list
- Morse fans 'better than inept poice'
- UK news in full

INTERNATIONAL NEWS
- US fears a copycat sniper as three die
- France's health boss quits over heat deaths
- Farc air attack on Colombian leader
- Schröder brings Wagner in from Nazi cold
- International news in full

OPINION
- Leader: Idi Amin's unfunny side
- Leader: Iraq's hostile neighbours
- Philip Johnston: Asylum dominates politics
- Adam Nicolson: Sin in the Outer Hebrides
- Opinion in full

CITY NEWS
- Accident Group chief points finger at HBOS
- Cazenove paves way for bigger payouts
- Westpac joins £2.5bn race for NBNZ
- Grubman still going in at Citigroup
- City news in full

SPORT
- Kirtley delivers for England
- Improved attitude was key
- Outsider details life inside Barnsley ranks
- Cumani revels in big league
- Sport in full

OBITUARIES
- Commander Stan Orr
- David Webster
- Chung Mong Hun

TELEGRAPH SERVICES
- Email bulletins
- Telegraph Promotions
- European Dailies Alliance

< PREVIOUS   ^ TOP

SPORT LATEST

Defensive duo out
Sol Campbell and Jonathan Woodgate will play no part in England's friendly against Croatia tomorrow night.

Henman unseeded for Open
British number one Tim Henman was not among the 32 seeds announced by the United States Tennis Association today.

- Football: Man City fined
- Gallery: Ins and outs
- Cricket: Live scoreboard
- Cricket: Text alerts
- Sport in full

Fantasy football is back
SIGN UP NOW CLICK HERE >>

TODAY'S FIXTURES
Football
International
Rep of Ireland v Australia (19.30)

Carling Cup
First Round
Stoke v Rochdale (19.45)

YESTERDAY'S RESULTS
Cricket
Third Npower Test Match
Final day of five
England v South Africa

FEATURES

Bear in the Arctic
The Everest climber takes on the high seas. Read his daily diary.

Lost in the wilderness
Gus Van Sant on his new movie, starring Matt Damon.

Bard attitude
Dominic Cavendish on Susannah York's Shakespearean show.

Ford and Ambridge
What cars would the The Archers drive?

Away with the fairies
Gavin Bell stays with Hansel and Gretel among Sweden's lakes.

How to obtain tax refunds
You can avoid some duties on holiday, but watch out for UK Customs when you come home.

Regal bore
Charles Spencer is underwhelmed by Edward II at the Globe.

Polly puts the metal on
Joe Muggs reviews P J Harvey at the Eden Project.

Lost in translation
David Gritten reviews Monty Python's Flying Circus.

The Pianist
Win a copy of Roman Polanski's film and a signed poster.

MATT

Alex

It is also true to say that site maps tend to be provided by the more complex sites, so there may be some mileage in trying to ascertain why Text 5 has a site map and Text 3 does not. Because of its origins in a complex print publication aimed at an audience that enjoys reading, telegraph.co.uk presents a complex array of possibilities for constructing a hyper-narrative within the site. There are the same repeated patterns of noun phrases as we found in Texts 3 and 4, in order to categorise the areas of the virtual building we might visit, but Text 5 goes further. It follows the well-known syntactic conventions of headline construction – although it is interesting to look at whether the conventions of web newspaper headlines are *precisely* the same as their print counterparts. Certainly, there seems to be the same degree of syntactic compression – omitted determiners (see Unit 1, pp. 7–20), conventionalised use of past **participles** and present tense verb forms. Often, though, there is some added detail in the headline that appears when you use the hyperlink and visit the article: so that, for example, '47 killed in Bombay' becomes 'Islam rebels blamed as bombs kill 47 in Bombay', introducing an extra clause.

Deliberate reference is made to the fact that the web and print editions of the newspaper are to a certain extent separately produced: stories from the print edition are listed as headlines only, whereas the breaking web stories give the opening sentence of the story as a taster. This makes explicit the assumption that web discourse and print discourse may be interrelated and to an extent mutually derived, but they are certainly not the same. Feature articles follow the headline with a summary of the article (rather than the opening paragraph), and they name the journalist who wrote the article – following a long-established tradition in print journalism that feature writers are named in the summary rather than in a byline.

As we have seen, then, most professionally produced sites will foreground the narrative possibilities on offer, placing them very prominently within their virtual reception area, and the linguistic strategies used to present these possibilities (or portals) will vary according to assumptions about audience and context of reception. Some more complex sites may even provide a thumbnail sketch of *all* of the narrative choices a reader might make, often with an eye on the traditions of web publishing.

Sometimes, though, there is a deliberate attempt to *conceal* the overall discourse structure of the site. A prime example of this is the hypertext novel – a form that pre-dates the Web, notably in the form of software tools for teaching children how to construct coherent written narrative. It was thought that the Web would popularise the hypertext novel, to the extent that the web form would rival the printed novel, but this has not happened to date.

As things stand, **authors** of hypertext novels have the option of providing them free on the Web, or publishing them on disk and charging for them. There is also the theoretical possibility of making them available via paid, password-protected access on the Web, but there appears to be no evidence of this happening. The closest, albeit poor, equivalent is the sale of **e-books** – downloadable versions of print publications.

To see an example of a genuine hypertext novel in action, go to http://www.waltersorrells.com/2.html. You should immediately notice that the narrative is not linear in the same sense as a printed novel. Once you have read to the bottom of the screen, there is no way out except to choose one of the hyperlinks on the page. Each hyperlink, as we have observed in relation to other types of web page, is either a noun phrase or a dynamic verb phrase (both very common carriers of lexical meaning in web hyperlinks); each hyperlink advances the narrative in subtly different ways. There is, however, the ever-present possibility of getting stuck in a loop: you keep seeing the same pages repeatedly, until you find a hyperlink that propels you down a linear route to the next cluster of nodes; then you navigate these nodes until you find another escape route. Each node typically provides some narrative development, but some only provide background or narrative reflection, so you learn more, or less, about each character, event and setting according to your chosen route through the plot. The entire reading experience is something unique to hypertext. Whether there will ever develop a novel form unique to the Web, exploiting the Web's conventions (which are *not* quite the same as other forms of hypertext), remains to be seen.

To return to our own central plot, though, the moral of this particular part of the story is that a site map is likely to be counter-productive to the aims of a hypertext novel; unless of course you wanted to display choices about where the reader could *enter* the narrative. It remains an underdeveloped form. The narrative challenge laid down by Laurence Sterne with *The Life and Opinions of Tristram Shandy* has been taken up but partially.

SUMMARY

One possible danger of thinking in metaphors is the temptation to believe that the metaphor is real, and lose sight of what is really happening to you. But, in a real sense, that is what the user interface is all about. In Unit one we looked at the desktop metaphor. Unit two has been an exploration of the default pages of websites, and the subtextual assumption that we are being tempted to explore the rest of the building. The word 'site' has a direct semantic link to a self-contained complex of buildings and the development of a website is routinely referred to as 'building' a site. From the default page we are frequently presented with only a single hyperlink labelled 'Enter'.

A website that contains nothing much at all, until the owner of it can clear enough space on their personal calendar to actually put something there, is given the designation 'under construction'; and if you are really lucky you might just get a friendly invitation to 'check back later' – as if the premises are currently vacant but someone might be moving in soon. However, where the site is not vacant, the linguistic patterns displayed in the foyer of the building summarise and foreground the narrative possibilities that are on offer to you, lying behind the doors that you can see leading to other parts of the building.

Extension

1   Collect more examples of front-of-house web pages that act as virtual reception areas, and attempt a similar analysis, trying to decide whether the underlying linguistic patterns vary significantly or whether a predictable pattern emerges. Pay particular attention to grammatical and pragmatic variation in relation to lexical content and levels of formality.

2   Try to develop other viable metaphors for exploring the discourse structure of websites. Conduct a survey of web users, gathering information about their perceptions of the browsing experience (where they imagine themselves to be when visiting a site), and see if any of your own metaphors appear in the data. Is there a persistent metaphorical model for web browsing, or is there significant variation in how people choose to embody it?

3   Make a detailed study into the use of syntactic and lexical patterns on the default pages of websites for different types of organisations – commercial and non-commercial. How do these patterns relate to assumptions about audience and context? This could begin with a study of the website for your own educational institution.

4   If you have access to an **intranet** website, use some of the concepts outlined in this unit to analyse some of its pages, and then compare them with the same institution's Internet website. Again, bear in mind the need to relate your findings to audience, context and encultured pragmatic meaning (subtext). Make sure that the data you gather from the intranet and Internet websites were **uploaded** at about the same time. In other words, avoid the scenario where the institution has just done a major overhaul of their Internet website but the intranet site is two years old and due for an overhaul next month.

Boundaries real and imagined: personal websites

Where a website is produced by an institution, there can be analogies with print publishing, because the site will not be published without being vetted by the institution. The real publishing revolution has come from the fact that *anyone* can put up their own site without, initially, having it vetted by anyone. Do personal **home pages** have a language of their own? This unit also looks at the technological context of personal websites.

HOW THE WEB DEFEATS BOUNDARIES

There is no doubt that personal websites will one day be important historical documents. They represent a sudden and profound democratisation of the publishing process that preserves a people's history in ways that not even the invention of analogue sound recording can rival. The difficulty for a linguist is how to classify them in relation to other forms and contexts of language use, given the wide variety of reasons why personal websites are published. We are used to the idea of political boundaries separating cultures, countries and, in some cases, languages. Until very recently, the technology used to communicate and to publish texts, within and across these boundaries, has been relatively easy to incorporate into the notion of self – personal identity, culture and nationality. To understand how the Web has blown all this apart, we need to be aware of the significance of one or two historical accidents.

If cigarettes had never been known, and an attempt were made now to develop and market something along similar lines, there is little doubt that it would not succeed. If we imagine a similar scenario with alcohol, it would very likely be banned and classified as a dangerous narcotic. However, if any company today were convinced that they could effectively prove exclusive ownership of the technology behind either cigarettes or alcohol, they would probably give it a try, as the revenue they could make from the licensing of the technology would be immense.

The same is true of the Internet: it contains a lot of potentially dangerous material, and if it was proposed as a new invention today, with prior knowledge of all its dangers, it would not be allowed to happen. But now that we have it, it has taken on a life of its own and is not owned by anyone. We are stuck with it, but if anyone could prove that they *owned* it, they would become very wealthy.

In 2000, an attempt was made by British Telecom to prove that they owned the underlying technology for hyperlinks in web pages, and, in a test case, they attempted to force a US Internet service provider, Prodigy, to pay them for use of the technology. If they had won the case, it would have had very far-reaching consequences for ISPs all over the world, and have put BT in the same league as Microsoft. But it was doomed to failure largely because it can be demonstrated that the idea and technology behind hypertext linking has been discussed and formulated by several people over the past several decades, dating as far back as 1944. Also, the overwhelming truth behind systems as complex as the Internet is that, because they rely on so many interconnecting technologies, it is impossible to prove intellectual ownership of the *entire* system.

As we saw in Unit one, of all the people on the planet who could possibly claim ownership of the World Wide Web, Tim Berners-Lee is the front runner. He has, however, publicly stated that he was not motivated by financial gain, but by the desire to improve communication and cooperation between people. He did envisage that people would probably have to pay for using the Web, but he appears not to have included himself in that financial equation. By historical good fortune, it was his system that gained prominence and became the international standard. Servers and browsers could plug in from anywhere on the planet, documents could be served to browsers across international borders, and the network grew outwards from a **backbone** that had essentially been developed in an academic environment and had been in existence many years before the Web was invented – thus providing a lot of built-in resistance to the forces of commercial exploitation.

There have been some attempts to close the browser market, so that only one browser will be the de facto standard. And by and large this has succeeded, nonetheless the concept of a web browser does remain an open standard, and alternatives do exist, so if you want to use a browser other than the one that came with your computer, you can: they are downloadable and mostly free. So, if the PC market ever opens up to alternative operating systems, you may see the spread of other browser software. The point here is that if someone develops their own web browser they are not infringing any copyright or intellectual property rights; and the only reason almost everyone uses the same browser currently is market saturation of a particular operating system.

PUBLISHING FOR EVERYONE

So, the very nature of the Internet (the network that the Web uses to exchange information) means that it would be nearly impossible for any one company to own the whole of it. The Web is like the airwaves: as long as you can find a frequency, you can broadcast. Extending this analogy, a potential broadcaster needs to apply for a licence from a regulatory body; these regulatory bodies are specific to individual countries and because of this will enforce different laws as a condition for granting a licence. Broadcasting without a licence is an offence in most circumstances and most countries. Once you have been granted a licence, you will need a large capital investment to buy the broadcasting equipment, and then a regular source of income to finance the broadcasts.

Another possible analogy is with print publishing. Unless you are prepared to finance the publication yourself, you will have to convince the publisher that it is worth their while investing money into printing and distributing your work. Even if you do finance your own print publication, there are national and international laws relating to exactly what you are allowed to publish.

Being a web publisher, then, is probably most like being able to broadcast globally without having to command large amounts of money or apply for a licence. Many websites still look much like printed documents because they contain written language and static pictures. Websites are different from all other media, however, because web publishing is not governed by national laws about the amount of 'traffic' or the type of content allowed within specific countries. All the other mass media, although they do have global potential, must conform to national regulatory laws – or face being shut down. This can of course happen to ISP accounts or even whole web servers: if the authorities do not like what you are publishing on the Web, they can have your Internet account cancelled, confiscate your computer or shut down the server that is publishing your material. But the big difference is that web servers are much harder to trace to geographical locations. Before anyone gets around to pulling the plug, you can make several perfect copies of your site and send them to the other side of the world, with very little chance of the new server being traced; you also do not need to be anywhere near the server in order to publish your material afresh. It is relatively simple to acquire another computer, another ISP account and some more web space on a server anywhere in the world: as something of a technological Hydra, the Web will re-grow severed heads fairly effortlessly. Also, because website viewing follows an **asynchronous** model, websites are much more difficult to detect than television or radio broadcasts. Print is an asynchronous medium too, but printed artefacts have a physical real-world existence: websites are infinitely more mercurial.

This is what many people see as the negative side of the Web – a haven for illicit activity where innocent surfers are in constant danger of stumbling across something very ugly. There is not the same sense of deliberate channel selection as there is with a TV or radio broadcast; print publications require a great deal of active seeking and physical handling, so with print too there are several stages at which you could opt out of the viewing process.

Many also hold the view that, if anyone can publish anything on the Web for next to nothing, where is the quality control? Quality control exists within organisations and within codes of practice related to commerce, but there is not much that determines or regulates what *individuals* choose to put on the Web. It is true to a certain extent that the presence of carefully researched academic papers, serious journalism, inventive entertainment and commerce, transmitted in the same medium as material that can clearly sometimes be either offensive or trivial – and this combined with the **hyperspace** phenomenon where you jump seamlessly from one to the other and back again – has a very strange effect. The legitimacy of web content is self-determining, rather than being imposed by external regulatory bodies: the very existence of the good stuff means that you hang out for it and ignore the rubbish. Commerce, academia and the arts have an interest in the Web maintaining a legitimised image: a kind of publishing for the people that benefits from the input of professionals.

DOES THE LANGUAGE OF WEBSITES EXIST?

While this book was in preparation, the author received some comments to the effect that there could not possibly be a language of websites, because people will use the same language on websites that they might use in diaries, newspaper articles, letters, short stories, shopping lists, casual conversations, etc. . . .

However, it is possible to isolate linguistic habits that broadly coincide with written **genres**, and it is possible to describe the forms and contextual motivations of speech – or even of restricted classes of electronic text such as SMS and chatroom conversations – but some would say that the heterogeneity of website material militates against finding meaningful, predictable linguistic patterns.

We established some linguistic patterns in relation to institutional websites in Units one and two, but it does perhaps become more difficult to establish reliable frameworks when analysing personal websites. What exactly are they? Electronic diaries? In that case, why not just type them into a word processor and save them on your own computer? Often personal websites are driven by the desire to record a specific personal interest: for example, the huge numbers of **fansites** for cult TV shows. But at the other end of the spectrum there are plenty of websites that do seem to be just personal reflection. Most will sit somewhere in between.

Personal websites appear to a curious hybrid of secret diary and public revelation. The personal facts and sentiments revealed are frequently more than many people would choose to reveal even in private conversations with friends, and yet they are there for the world to see. A useful analogy is this: a dense forest where a personal diary is hidden underneath a tree; the diarist returns to the same spot to update the diary every day. Given the size and heavily wooded nature of the forest, it is perhaps unlikely that many people would read the diary. There is, however, the thrill of knowing that someone just *might* read it – and, crucially, read it anonymously without personal consequences to the diarist. What is more, the diary is charmed so that it can only be moved, altered or destroyed by the person who wrote it.

Activity

It is not possible in any single publication to reflect upon or even begin to survey a representative sample of all the possible types of personal expression that can appear on the Web. The aim of this activity is only to begin an exploration of how such expression is achieved linguistically.

Text 6: Me, Myself and Mon, Text 7: blogumentary and Text 8; Foruta are different examples of websites being used for personal expression, not funded or legitimised by any kind of commercial organisation. In other words, the publishing process is a purely personal venture in each case, and any costs involved have been borne by the individual.

The websites vary considerably in purpose. In Text 6 the Web is being used almost entirely as a medium for the presentation of self; Text 7 is a **weblog** – a kind of online diary popularised by services such as blogger.com; Text 8 is the home page of an amateur rock band managed by a teenager.

1   Are there any key grammatical, lexical or semantic patterns that you think characterise this kind of writing and mark it out as a variety distinct from other kinds of web writing? You may want to look carefully at pronouns and **deictic** features.

2   Which features of graphology and page design are worthy of comment, possibly by comparison with the examples we have looked at in Units one and two?

3   Do any of the texts have hidden messages or agendas that are perhaps not openly stated in the language of the text? One possible way into this is to try to describe any linguistic strategies that the authors of the pages are using (consciously or unconsciously) to present their own personalities.

4   Try to give at least some tentative thought to the question of whether we can we apply the traditional text analysis concepts of audience and purpose to these texts. Even if it is sometimes not clear who the texts are aimed at, are they dealing with a **notional**, imagined audience? How do we apply the concept of contextual motivation, given that any imagined audience is not **co-present**?

Me, Myself and Mon

Last updated: 10/04/2003

My Photo Album

My Info:

Name: Chanoknart Athakravi

Email: chanoknart@yahoo.com

chanoknart@athakravi.com

NaturalOfrequency@hotmail.com

ICQ number: 126264898

The purpose of this page is for my friends around the world to keep in touch with me when I am with my family in Thailand, and for my family in Thailand to keep in touch when I am with my friends in England!!!

My name is Chanoknart Athakravi, or Mon as most people call me although some other nick names do exist such as Mona, Monica, Cat etc... I'm originally from Thailand but spending most of the year in England studying here, in Oxford (no, not at THE Oxford university).

I was born on the 17th of September 1983 as the first of my generation and the first child of the first child of my grandparents, then the rest of us followe!

My aim in life, at the moment is to survive this course to become the person who make arts and sciences meet, an architect! Very hard for a person with nonexistant brain like me.

Links:

Athakravi family page

My friends at Benenden

My design and Technology page

My hobbies are quite odd - as my friends would say. This is when it really clashes! I do basketball, tennis, golf, squash, badminton, horse-riding and... wait for it... piano, flute, Thai musical instruments, Ballroom dancing, Latin dancing, Modern dance and I bake!

Me at the Moment

Hello! How are you all? It's the second week of the Easter Holiday at the moment, and I'm already back here in Oxford, working on the holiday project and reading for the exam which is on the first week of next term!

Oh, on good news, I'm moving to the Manchester School of Architecture next year, they've given me an unconditional offer for year 2 so I'm definitely going! This is just going to be a life savior for me! (Not saying anything against the Oxford one where I'm currently at!) So I'll be looking around for somehwere to live pretty soon, for September!

My grades from last term are coming out on Monday, wish me luck! Just aiming for a pass really, not expecting anything much more than that because the portfolio is not that great, now that I've come to think of it! Could have done much better.

After the busy term I've finally had some time to go out with my friend here. Was her birthday yesterday and we went out for some Thai food and I made her a little cake (didn't know what to give her as a present so I thought that's the easiest option!)

By the way, you guys back there be careful ok? Don't catch the SARS 'cause it's sooooooooo scary, don't want to have anyone I know catching it at all. Take a very, very good care of yourselves!

Text 7: blogumentary

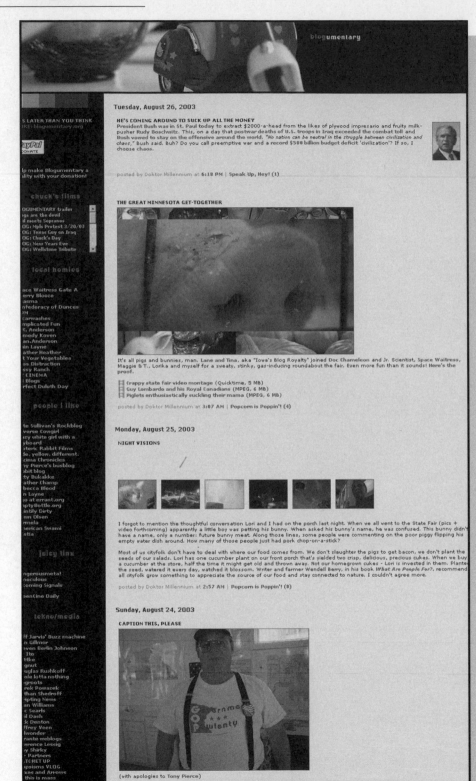

blogumentary

Tuesday, August 26, 2003

HE'S COMING AROUND TO SUCK UP ALL THE MONEY

President Bush was in St. Paul today to extract $2000-a-head from the likes of plywood impresario and fruity milk-pusher Rudy Boschwitz. This, on a day that postwar deaths of U.S. troops in Iraq exceeded the combat toll and Bush vowed to stay on the offensive around the world. *"No nation can be neutral in the struggle between civilization and chaos,"* Bush said. Buh? Do you call preemptive war and a record $500 billion budget deficit 'civilization'? If so, I choose chaos.

posted by Doktor Millennium at 6:18 PM | Speak Up, Hey! (1)

THE GREAT MINNESOTA GET-TOGETHER

It's all pigs and bunnies, man. Lane and Tina, aka "Iowa's Blog Royalty" joined Doc Chameleon and Jr. Scientist, Space Waitress, Maggie & T., Lorika and myself for a sweaty, stinky, gas-inducing roundabout the fair. Even more fun than it sounds! Here's the proof.

- Crappy state fair video montage (Quicktime, 5 MB)
- Guy Lombardo and his Royal Canadians (MPEG, 6 MB)
- Piglets enthusiastically suckling their mama (MPEG, 6 MB)

posted by Doktor Millennium at 3:07 AM | Popcorn is Poppin'! (4)

Monday, August 25, 2003

NIGHT VISIONS

I forgot to mention the thoughtful conversation Lori and I had on the porch last night. When we all went to the State Fair (pics + video forthcoming) apparently a little boy was petting his bunny. When asked his bunny's name, he was confused. This bunny didn't have a name, only a number: future bunny meat. Along those lines, some people were commenting on the poor piggy flipping his empty water dish around. How many of those people just had pork chop-on-a-stick?

Most of us cityfolk don't have to deal with where our food comes from. We don't slaughter the pigs to get bacon, we don't plant the seeds of our salads. Lori has one cucumber plant on our front porch that's yielded two crisp, delicious, precious cukes. When we buy a cucumber at the store, half the time it might get old and thrown away. Not our homegrown cukes - Lori is invested in them. Planted the seed, watered it every day, watched it blossom. Writer and farmer Wendell Berry, in his book *What Are People For?*, recommend all cityfolk grow something to appreciate the source of our food and stay connected to nature. I couldn't agree more.

posted by Doktor Millennium at 2:57 AM | Popcorn is Poppin'! (8)

Sunday, August 24, 2003

CAPTION THIS, PLEASE

(with apologies to Tony Pierce)

posted by Doktor Millennium at 7:56 PM | Popcorn is Poppin'! (13)

S LATER THAN YOU THINK
RE: blogumentary.org

PayPal
DONATE

lp make Blogumentary a
ality with your donation!

chuck's films

OGUMENTARY trailer
gs are the devil
il meets Sopranos
OG: Mpls Protest 3/20/03
OG: Texas Guy on Iraq
OG: Chuck's Day
OG: New Years Eve
OG: Wellstone Tribute

local homies

ace Waitress Gate A
erry Blooze
asma
nfederacy of Dunces
JM
carwashes
mplicated Fun
T. Anderson
medy Koven
an.Anderson
in Layne
ather Heather
t Your Vegetables
ss Distraction
essy Ranch
CINEMA
l Blogs
rfect Duluth Day

people i like

te Sullivan's Rockblog
verse Cowgirl
zy white girl with a
yboard
oteric Rabbit Films
de. yellow. different.
zima Chronicles
ry Pierce's busblog
abit blog
ty Bukakke
ather Champ
becca Blood
n Layne
io at errant.org
ptyBottle.org
inbly Dirty
wn Olsen
mela
merican Swami
stia

juicy linx

ngerousmeta!
noculous
coming Signals

eentine Daily

tekno/media

ff Jarvis' Buzz machine
n Gillmor
even Berlin Johnson
lfo
ttle
gnut
uglas Rushkoff
ole lotta nothing
groots
rek Powazek
than Shedroff
pting News
an Williams
c Searls
l Dash
k Denton
ffrey Veen
iwonder
ranta weblogs
wrence Lessig
y Shirky
- Partners
TCHET UP
ipsioms VLOG
xes and Arrows
this is mass
mmunication?
t Online Journalism Review
stitute for New Media
dies

foruta

NEWS

NEWS
BAND
RELEASES
GIGS
PICTURES
AUDIO
VIDEO
BOARD
MERCHANDISE
CONTACT
LINKS

Message from Mark

"Hey gang, just a quick update on the state of play, Nick S. is not in the country at the moment, and I'm off for a week on friday, but a week on saturday Foruta is back in the UK and ready to play a load of gigs and write a few new songs for the album, which will have the greatest cover and title of all time... guarenteed. Me and Nick have been giggling like school girls at work thinking about this! Ok, stay tuned!"

Foruta win Youth Arts Festival

Foruta won the Glusburn Institute Youth Arts Festival tonight and are playing at Tadcaster Grammar School in front of upto 3000 people on July 5th. They've been away for a while but it seems they are back in full force. Also be sure not to miss the gigs in Leeds on 26th and 30th June.

Peroufest video

Foruta's full set from Peroufest 2003 is now available on the Peroufest video, they played 8 songs (including all 5 from the untitled ep), email comfortinsound@btinternet.com for a copy.

Gig cancelled

The Packhorse gig on Monday has been cancelled. The date will be rescheduled for the summer. The Joseph's Well videos are online now for your viewing pleasure, just jump to the video section.

Monday's videos

If you missed Foruta on Monday at Joseph's Well (or even if you didn't) you can watch videos of the entire gig on the video section. The set includes two new songs, 'Call It A Democracy' and 'Destroy Me'.

New merchandise

The new merchandise is finally here, so go spend some money!

New gig date

Foruta have just been confirmed to return to Joseph's Well on June 30th supporting Fat Abbot.

New merchandise

New merchandise is coming this week so keep your eyes peeled for some swish new stuff.

Buy the ep online

Go to the merchandise section to buy the Unitled EP online for £5.

New website opened...

The new foruta website is here. Make sure you catch foruta live this month at Bradford Empress (Sat 5th), Joseph's Well in Leeds (Mon 7th), Embsay Village Hall (Wed 16th) and Leeds Packhorse (21st).

Website by Tom Perou.

Commentary

In most texts, pronouns and deictic features are very closely related to assumptions about audience and context. For example, the pronoun 'you' is used in a different way by each of the three texts. Text 8 is addressing a specific audience of people who may have visited the site for news of the band's activities: this is reinforced by context-dependent nouns that will only be meaningful to people who already follow the band – 'Peroufest', for example. In Text 8, the pronoun 'you' is generic in that the writer does not know the individual identities of the people that the message is aimed at, but it also shares some of the pragmatic **force** present when the same pronoun is used in either one-to-one spoken interaction or a public lecture.

Text 7 uses the 'you' pronoun in an entirely generic way (in the same way that speakers and writers of most dialects of English are forced into, because there is no unique form for the generic pronoun in English): 'Do you call pre-emptive war' could be expressed 'Does one call pre-emptive war'. This suggests that the author of Text 7 is anticipating a wider audience – casual surfers, and people who are interested in reading web diaries. This author has not compartmentalised the audience to the same extent as the author of Text 8.

Moving on to Text 6, this text foregrounds its purpose from the opening sentence, so that when we come across the 'you' pronoun in the bottom part of the page it is clear that author is addressing a specific group of people known personally to them.

It is common for personal websites to include deictic reference using demonstrative adjectives such as 'this' and adverbs such as 'here' and 'there'. These are part of a deictic strategy that references the concept of space in two different ways – the physical environment that the author inhabits while writing the page, and the virtual space of the page itself. Text 7 makes the least use of this kind of duality, instead working within a frame that is more like a seamless spectrum extending from the author's personal living space to international politics and intertextual references – hence phrases like 'on the porch', 'around the world' and 'in his book' on the same page, without any **transitional markers** other than date entries, sub-headings or paragraph breaks. This is partly a convention of weblogs, but also partly a reflection of the site as a means of exploring ideas and musing on experience rather than promoting the personality of the author.

Text 8 makes more use of the duality of real and virtual space, using the adverb 'online' to refer to the virtual space where information about the band can be found, and locating the narrative of the band's activities within real time and space by using the names of physical venues and organised events.

Text 6 is perhaps a good example of a purely personal website, with its reference to virtual and real space being expressed less ambiguously by 'this page', 'Thailand', 'Oxford' and 'Manchester'. The author locates herself in time and space with a mini-biography and descriptions of future events, attempting to reconcile the physical distance between herself and her friends and family by using virtual space to collate reflections about them.

Graphologically, Text 6 has several features worthy of comment. The typeface Comic Sans MS, used for the heading, is very popular because it signifies a kind of middle ground between print and handwriting. The audience is aware that the characteristics of the medium mean that the heading cannot have been handwritten, but sparing use of the sub-class known as **handwriting fonts** can have the effect of shifting the register of the page towards either intimacy or light-heartedness. (There is a growing use of Comic Sans MS in internal memos and PowerPoint presentations within institutions, in order to **ameliorate** the pragmatic force of management directives and make management seem more friendly and approachable.)

Text 6 also makes graphologically explicit the distinction between biographical background and more recent events: the general personality sketch at the top of the page is in a sans serif font, whereas the more up-to-date information at the bottom is in a serif font (probably the default for the software being used to create the page). This does not relate to professional printing practice, but simply to the author's desire to visually differentiate the two types of information, reinforced by the ruled line between the two sections of the page. As we saw in Unit one (pp. 7–20), the development of typography in web publishing diverged from the traditions of print publishing at an early stage.

The use of a graphical background in Text 6 is a stylistic device that only took off properly in amateur websites. It is actually a single image, and there is an instruction in the code of the page that tells the browser to tile it repeatedly underneath any other textual or graphical content on the page. This highlights a key difference between personal and institutional sites, in terms of the **semiotic** relationship between text and graphics. Institutional sites must carry linguistic content in a form that is easily decoded, or the site fails to accomplish its institutional purpose. Personal pages are constructed more according to the principles of private living space, and so there can be greater experimentation with different types of communication. The virtual space is decorated in the same way that we might decorate the interior of a room: if a visitor to the room notices text on the walls and has to concentrate on filtering out the background in order to read the text, then so be it, because the context of reception allows more time to be spent on the decoding process. Thus, we can argue that personal

47

web pages are aesthetic objects in a way that is only secondary when constructing institutional sites.

Personal websites are often a curious inversion of the concept of privacy – private thoughts constructed in virtual space as a kind of electronic security blanket. A different way of looking at the same idea would be to see it as a sculpture put together from collected parts ('bricolage' as Daniel Chandler (1998), after Claude Lévi-Strauss (1974), has called it), with some original text overlaid to **anchor** the meaning. Again, the best example of this, from the three we are looking at, would be Text 6.

As Daniel Chandler (1998) has commented, some weblogs contain statements and reflections that the author may not be inclined to share during even one-to-one conversational contexts with peers or family members. And yet the author *is* prepared to publish them in a medium where potentially they could be read by millions of people globally. One notable example of this is http://katdennings.com, where a celebrity has chosen to record her inner thoughts with no other motive than simply wanting to express them. The subtext of many personal pages is partly the security blanket phenomenon outlined above, but partly also the sense that the author does not believe many people will read the page – while at the same time *daring* it to achieve a global profile.

DOPPELGÄNGER: YOUR WEB PERSONALITY

Following Daniel Chandler's (1998) work, based on the premise that personal websites are about constructing and expressing identity in ways that we would not consider during **synchronous** interaction, we can speculate that if the dare ever came true and the site became well known and talked about, the author might be slightly alarmed.

Weblogs (from which the contracted form **blog** and the name of the popular service blogger.com are derived) are a form of self-expression that Rebecca Blood (2000) has identified as taking two forms. There are **filter-style** weblogs where the author presents some information about themselves and their interests, and then devotes most of the site to listing links to external sites that the author values highly because they have found them useful themselves or because they reflect their own values and interests. Thus, the author is able to present a gateway carefully designed to filter out most web content and only allow access to a very heavily edited version of the Web. In linguistic terms, this could be seen as a discourse **gatekeeper**, a large hypertext node where the hyperlinks are periodically reviewed, rewiring the narrative pathways that the filter will allow according to the subtext the author wants to embody.

This differs from the weblog subcategory that Rebecca Blood calls the blogger type, which is much more like a traditional diary. The narrative is linear and divided up into date entries. Unlike a handwritten diary, there is not as much pressure to make an entry for *every* calendar day, because these do not present themselves as blank pages if they are not used. A paper diary presents a narrative template that exerts pragmatic pressure on the owner to fill it with events, reflections or **mnemonic** cues related to forthcoming events. But a blog has as part of its underlying concept a selectivity that allows the user to miss out whole segments of time, in this way forging new **syntagmatic** relations between the experiences chosen for presentation. In other words, a blog is *meant* to be selective. Old pages are typically archived in date order and hyperlinks to the archive included as part of the page. The active part of the page contains only the most recent entries. A blog can share some discourse features with web-based newspaper reporting, where key noun phrases are marked as hyperlinks to internal or external pages that explore the referenced concept in more detail. Text 7 routinely makes use of this technique.

Another aspect of Daniel Chandler's (1998) thinking on personal websites is that they present an essentially altered self. It is a version of ourselves that we construct for the consumption of an unknown public – which may consist of only one person or as many as half a million people. The narrative voice very often presents itself as if it is involved in one-to-one interaction with an imaginary individual. Having constructed it, we do not necessarily want to confront it, but we can exercise the privilege of revising it and overwriting older versions of our web personality, sometimes choosing to leave the older versions buried in a weblog archive.

Daniel Chandler points out that this presupposes a very changeable version of the personality, working against the **modernist** idea that the personality is stable throughout all experience and that we are just trying to find it and be true to it; and instead reinforcing the **post-modernist** assumption that the personality is constantly being redefined.

Some types of analysis of conversational interaction have focused on the concept of **face** – for example, positive face and negative face in relation to politeness. The assumption is that in synchronous personal interaction the participants frequently revise the concept of self, erasing

49

and rewriting our personalities according to social and linguistic context. We have said that personal web page writing is asynchronous, but it does often take on some features of conversational language when the author speaks to their imagined audience of one. An example of this is the use of unfinished **adjacency pairs**, as in the question 'How are you all?' in Text 6. No reply will be received in the immediate context of asking the question, but in a synchronous spoken conversation the question might receive a standard response like 'Fine' or 'Very well'. The fact that the adjacency pair is not actually a finished pair but has an imagined or empty response, allows a great deal of fluidity in how the author's **persona** is perceived by the audience: the individual viewer consciously or unconsciously fills in the other half of the adjacency pair – because there is a relatively restricted set of socialised completions to choose from.

SUMMARY

This unit has demonstrated that many of the established linguistic frameworks used for analysing spoken and written language in the second half of the twentieth century can be applied effectively to personal websites – if we just remember that they are contextually motivated texts comparable to other, older genres yet revolutionary in the patterns of pragmatic meaning that they are capable of conveying. As we have seen, one very useful way into these meanings is to look at Daniel Chandler's (1998) notion of identity, and how a version of identity can be constructed, one that the author is motivated to both publish and, paradoxically, keep private at the same time. The Web is a relatively new medium, and it does have a tendency to propagate an image of itself as entirely global and entirely democratic. As Marshall McLuhan (2001 [1967]) famously pointed out in the 1960s, a communication medium primarily carries a message about how important the medium *itself* is, and how it is so powerful that civilisation cannot manage without it – 'the medium is the message'. It is certainly true that the myth of global access to the Internet is just that – a myth, propagated by Western commercial interests – but it is becoming more of a reality as time goes on, and the linguistic heterogeneity of the Web is examining itself and the real world in ever more interesting ways.

1   Collect URLs and printouts of blogger-style weblogs published by authors of different genders and ethnic backgrounds. Note any interesting linguistic patterns that you find, and say whether there is any correlation between gender or ethnic background and stylistic or pragmatic features.

2   Keep printouts of selected filter-style weblogs, and monitor how the links are updated or changed over a period of time. Analyse the grammatical and lexical patterns in the hyperlinks used to link to the external sites, exploring how these linguistic patterns can be linked to the identities of the authors.

3   Analyse features of graphology and layout in a range of different personal websites. How far are these features related to the age and technical background of the author?

Streamers and flashers: sound and video content on the Web

Many people think that we are moving ever closer to a time when the Web, television, radio, newspapers and telephones will all merge into one device. At the moment the Web is a somewhat uneasy, fragile hybrid of all of these functions. This being the case, how do we apply analytical frameworks to websites that offer **multimedia** content, and what else to we need to know about technology in order to achieve this analysis?

THE DIGITAL REVOLUTION

The difference between digital and analogue is often confused and misunderstood, but it is at the heart of how the Web has begun to come of age in recent years. What has this got to with the language of websites? Every mass medium manifests changes in linguistic content because of changing technology: the coincidence of developments in digital audio-visual technology with the growth of the Web signals the Web's transition from what some would see as an electronic 'people's printing press' into a mass medium that rivals the cinema, television, radio, print and telecommunications – while combining aspects of all of these and synthesising something entirely new.

Computers are digital. They need instructions that consist of digits only – 0 and 1. The instructions can be vastly complex, but they must have strings of only 0 and 1 in them. If you try to introduce ambiguity – information that could be a 0 but could, in other cultural contexts, be seen as 1, a computer will reject it or fail to process it. It is misleading to use the term 'brain' to refer to the computer's **processor** because unlike our own brains the processor is only capable of handling one kind of information – electrical signals that represent 0 or 1.

There has been a massive amount of commentary in recent years about the digital revolution. Although computers have been affecting the way we live since at least the Second World War, the digital revolution only began to take hold in the 1980s. Before that, the world of sound and audio-visual reproduction was analogue, and the devices we used in everyday life were controlled by analogue systems. Perhaps the most well-known chapter in the digital revolution was the introduction of the Compact Disc (CD) in the early 1980s. Until then, pre-recorded music had been sold predominantly in the form of phonograph records, which were made of shellac in the early twentieth century, but more recently were, and still are, made of vinyl, a tougher, more flexible material. The technology of records remained unchanged in principle from their earliest forms to their decline in the late 1980s and early 1990s, and still remains unchanged, now that the format is enjoying a renaissance as a minority interest; it has also been the mainstay of dance music culture in a relatively unbroken tradition.

Very simply, a record has a continuous spiral groove that starts at the outside of the circle and moves in towards the middle. The groove is like a valley with uneven bumps on the bottom. Every bump has been put there by a cutter in the factory, and every bump matches up to a small part of the music. When the record is played, a needle rests in the groove, and a motor turns the record on a flat surface at an even speed. Each time the needle goes over a bump, a signal is sent to an amplifier and you hear the bump through the speakers. Hearing the signals from the bumps, in the right order and at the right speed, means that you are hearing the music played back to you. Thus, the sequence of bumps is an analogue of the music.

The problem is that new bumps get introduced into the groove almost as soon as the record is taken out of its sleeve for the first time. A spec of dust, a hair, some dried liquid on the surface of the record, a scratch on the surface of the record, will all create new bumps in the groove and be heard through the speakers when you play the record. This is a side effect of analogue recording technology: it cannot select out and ignore material that should not be there. A computer, however, can only deal with information encoded as 1 and 0: it can do nothing with dust or hair or scratches. If there are enough scratches to stop the digits from getting through, the music will just stop.

Digital technology works very differently. For example, a CD player shines a laser light on to the surface of the CD and reads the reflection. If it can read the digits in the expected way, it sends the information as a signal to the amplifier, and ignores everything else. In the late 1980s, when the home PC became a reality in the form we are familiar with today, sound recording had been in existence in digital form (the form that the PC can make use of) for several years.

IT'S ALIVE: MULTIMEDIA CONTENT

Digital audio, the raw material of a music CD, can just as easily be stored on a computer **hard disk** or **floppy disk**, so, when the PC arrived, the potential for it to deal in more than written text was already there. It was not long before basic **sound cards** became available and the PC was on its way to becoming a multimedia device.

We can now fast forward to the mid-1990s when the Web was beginning to take off: digital sound recording was the norm; vinyl had 'died' as a medium for the general release of pop music. Hard disks in home PCs had become significantly bigger and capable of storing moderate amounts of digital audio. And digital video was in its infancy as a medium accessible to home users, but it had been in use in the film industry for several years. Sequences of moving images, which for many years the home user had been able to record onto video tape, could now be stored in digital form on a hard disk, but the huge file sizes involved in storing and manipulating digital video meant that the average home user would be excluded from this area for several years to come.

An important advantage of digital information over analogue is that the parts of the message the computer does not need can be

55

stripped out. All information in the analogue domain contains **redundancy**. For example, an analogue recording of a piece of music contains a lot of information that the human ear cannot hear. If the recording is digital, this redundant information can be stripped out and the recording can be **compressed**. The same applies to video. An analogue video recording contains, for example, information about colour that can be significantly reduced without the human eye noticing the difference. The ability to compress video signals in this way was largely responsible for the explosion in the number of TV channels available worldwide in the late 1990s.

In 1995, the Xing Technology Corporation brought the Web into the multimedia dimension by inventing a protocol that allowed a process over the Web called streaming. Essentially, this involves downloading audio and video files in the same way that you would download a text-based web page. The differences, however, are: video and audio are **real time** media that need to be viewed in a continuous linear sequence, rather that being scanned and re-scanned as a single static entity (like written language); a full file would be too big to fit on most users' hard disks; and a full file would take too long to download at 1995 connection speeds, even if it were compressed. Streaming allows small parts of the file to be received in a continuous sequence, a stream. This is very like the way a television receives signals through the air, but with the slow dial-up connections of the mid-1990s there was a good chance of the connection suddenly slowing down or even being dropped altogether. For this reason, a small part of the stream is **buffered** to the hard disk. This is a way of having a kind of 'reserve tank' of data that can be used to supplement the data stream if the connection is temporarily broken. At time of writing, streaming technology is still largely unchanged. The only tangible difference is that connection speeds have increased, allowing larger, higher-quality video and audio files to be streamed.

In 1999, Xing was acquired by RealNetworks. RealPlayer was the first widely used browser plug-in for viewing and listening to streamed media. Developing in parallel to it was Windows Media Player that ships as part of the Microsoft Windows operating system. The other major participator in the streaming media plug-in market is QuickTime Player, developed initially and primarily for Apple machines but now widely available for the PC **platform** too. These three software plug-in players have now become the de facto alternatives when choosing to experience streamed media via the Web. There is a limited amount of compatibility between them, but recent developments have meant increasingly that, as each of the formats vies for control of the market, the user really needs to have all three players installed and make sure that the version of each one is up to date. Some sites will do an automatic check of your system and download and install the latest versions for you.

Activity

'This is not a Love Song', written by Simon Beaufoy and directed by Bille Eltringham, was the first film to be streamed via the Web simultaneously with its release in UK cinemas on 5 September 2003. It was also streamed into selected cinemas, rather than being shown on the conventional medium of 35 mm film. So, the film makes use of web technology for mainstream viewing, in multiple contexts, in a unique and innovative way.

Text 9: This is not a Love Song, is a screenshot taken from the web presence and viewing portal for the film – http://www.thisisnotalovesong. com. From this site, the film could either be streamed or downloaded for **offline** viewing. The site also contains general publicity information about the film.

1   How does the language used on this page reflect an awareness of the multiple contexts in which the film can be viewed? Does any of the linguistic content demonstrate a response to changing context?

2   How do the grammatical and lexical patterns compare with other types of website that we have encountered in the first three units?

3   Comment on how space, colour and typography contribute to the visual style of the page. (You will need access to the Internet in order to see the page in its original colour.)

4   Comment on the significance of the title 'This is not a love song' and how it is echoed grammatically throughout the page.

Text 9: This is not a Love Song

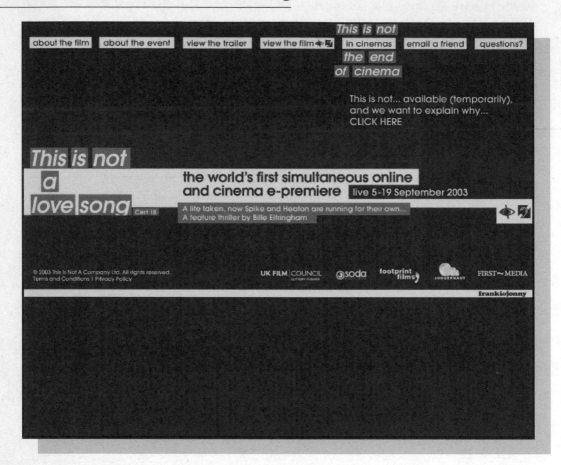

Commentary

Much of the page hinges around the repeated phrase 'This is not', an unfinished **subject-verb** unit that combines with a negative particle to produce a syntactic expectation of either a noun phrase, an adjective or a **non-finite** verb form. At a simple level, this is a direct echo of the syntactic structure of the title, but there are differences in how this echo is created, and how context is anticipated.

Each of the six white bars showing black text across the top of the page is a hyperlink. In the same way as the front-of-house concept that we looked at in Unit two (pp. 21–36), these hyperlinks offer narrative possibilities related to the function of the institution. This time, though, the institution is a film rather than an organisation: organisations are involved in the production and distribution of the film, but the focus of the site is the film itself. A film is an example of a **media text,** which will usually achieve a high public profile for a limited period, using an official site as a medium for publicity during the theatrical, rental and purchase releases of the film. This potentially transient nature of the film as an 'institution', rather than the relatively permanent presence of a company website, for example, has an effect on the discourse structure of the page.

It is also fair to say that the site holds an awareness of the unique nature of the broadcasting event, and that this is reflected linguistically. The inter-textuality between the film and the website is foregrounded in subtle ways, to a greater extent than most official movie sites (most of which are tied in to **merchandising** in one way or another).

◎ You will need access to the web page itself in order to see the following features properly.

When the mouse is moved over each of the hyperlinks at the top of the page, a sentence beginning 'This is not' appears as white text on red bars around the hyperlink. The red bars are animated and appear to bounce before settling into place so that they can be read, mirroring the behaviour of the central textual and graphical elements when the page is first loaded. Animating in this way is achieved using **Macromedia Flash,** a software plug-in that has also played a part in extending the functionality of the Web beyond simple HTML.

It is impossible to show all of the Flash animations on this web page in a screenshot, but in order of appearance from left to right they are: 'This is not Hollywood'; 'This is not conventional'; 'This is not the whole film'; 'This is not a multiplex'; 'This is not the end of cinema'; 'This is not junk mail'; and 'This is not a problem'. The verb forms are interesting, because as strict non-finite forms they are missing the word 'to': this use of the root form to signal a course of action initiated by a physical act comes originally from labels on switches for operating machines, but it has pervaded the Web as a convention for labelling hyperlinks. The most obvious link between the Flash text and the hyperlink label is a semantic one, antici-pating and answering possible issues that might arise before or during the choosing of the hyperlink; only in one case is there repetition of a lexeme from the label.

At the level of discourse structure, it would also be possible to see each coupling of white hyperlink label and Flash text as a kind of conver-sational **exchange**. If we imagine a spoken enquiry that begins with 'About

59

the film . . .', we could also imagine 'This is not Hollywood' as a reply. Such an exchange assumes a lot of unspoken contextual awareness, to the extent that, for example, the deictic force of the **demonstrative** pronoun 'this' is not clear – but this kind of dynamic is fairly typical of a new kind of adjacency pair developing out of the relationship between hyperlink labels and the explanatory text appearing as the mouse hovers over them.

Anticipation is the key. The title of the movie suggests that it is anticipating expectations of genre and setting up the suggestion that it sits outside comfortable definitions of genre; while the supporting linguistic content of the page underlines the unique technical way in which multiple viewing contexts have been handled. An analysis of the noun phrase in the centre of the page bears this out. Announcements of future events on publicly displayed notices often centre on a single noun phrase, because a single noun phrase is easier to decode quickly than a complete sentence. However, the unprecedented, multiple contexts of the 'This is not a Love Song' première require the noun phrase to be very heavily loaded lexically so that all of the key information is encoded. An added burden comes from the fact that post-modified noun phrases are less easy to decode than pre-modified noun phrases, so the end result here is a noun phrase with a lexically dense pre-modifying unit.

The semantic distinctions that need to be encoded are: that the broadcast is a première; that it is being shown in cinemas at the same time as being streamed via the Web; that the main emphasis is on the electronic nature of the première; and that it is the first time this has been done anywhere in the world. Part of this meaning is handled morphologically in the head noun: by analogy with the noun 'e-mail', the **prefix** morpheme {e-} has come to signify an electronic or virtual version of an event more traditionally performed in the physical world, an example from the language of mobile phones being 'e-topup'.

Another technique used to squeeze extra meaning into the pre-modifying phrase is to use a **genitive** form of a noun phrase as a determiner – 'the world's'. This is followed by a triple **adjective cluster** – 'first simultaneous online' – and then a conjunction that allows the pairing of 'online' with 'cinema' as concepts with equal status and prominence in defining the type of première being publicised. The word 'online' originally referred to electrical signals being sent and received, with more specific reference in recent years to data communications. So a modem is described as 'online' when it successfully linked to another modem, however the meaning has become **widened** to include any activity that takes place via the Internet. An example of this is 'online gaming' which usually involves dedicated gaming software with the ability to join the Internet and invite other connected users (running the same software) to join in. The word 'cinema' was originally a noun, but is now commonly used as an adjective through a process called **functional shift**.

This ability to cram multiple pre-modifiers in before the head noun is symptomatic of English. English allows, subject to human memory, an almost limitless string of **adjectival** or **nominal** pre-modifiers before the head of a noun phrase. If the same phrase were translated into French, it would almost certainly have to include several **sub-clauses** as post-modifiers. If it were translated into German, there would very likely be several **neologisms** created by the **compounding** of **free morphemes**. Does this mean English is a more natural web language than some others, because of its tendency towards compressed noun phrases of the type illustrated above? Where instantaneous decoding of lexical meaning and semantic relations is important, in the instant where the casual surfer decides whether to stay at that page or hit the Back button, perhaps the English noun phrase structure offers the kind of condensed linguistic code that web designers need.

Black space, as well as being a minimalist design feature, is used to respond to changing events in very much the same way as we saw on the Salford University site in Unit two (pp. 21–36). The spatial rhythm of the overall page design is disrupted in order to foreground what the news media refer to as 'breaking news'. Repetition of the key phrase 'This is not . . .' adds a light-hearted, gently ironic stance in order to soften the pragmatic blow of the movie being temporarily unavailable. Careful management of tone is needed, in view of the fact that this development temporarily means the site is promoting a product that cannot be obtained.

This in turn raises the whole issue of demand in relation to transmission of media texts. No other medium responds incrementally to increased demand by attempting to increase the volume of its output until eventually the technical infrastructure ceases to function. Television and radio broadcasting operate at a predetermined capacity: the home viewer cannot affect the transmitter by simply turning on another TV set. Similarly, sales of newspapers in a newsagent do not immediately link back to the newspaper office and make the printing press run faster. But every new user who visits a website will increase the activity of that web server; the server will try to send pages for every new user, and if it exceeds its safe **bandwidth** it will begin to slow down and eventually stop responding to new users, or worse stop functioning altogether and **crash**.

An aspect of the way the social psyche responds to websites, as compared with TV or print, is that this kind of overloading is seen as acceptable or even normal: the Web still has a reputation as inherently unreliable, and users have a high level of tolerance to this. This originates partly in the accepted notion that computers themselves are unreliable, vulnerable and precariously balanced.

A **pop-up window** uses the concept of disrupted spatial rhythm to indicate a temporary response to unforeseen events. On the 'This is not a Love Song' site, clicking the link related to the temporary technical problem will spawn a new window with the explanation in full to be read and scrolled through. In itself, the spawning of new windows for new pages, as opposed to loading the new page in the same window, provides an added dimension to the discourse of hypertext, because it then becomes possible to have several narrative threads on the go at the same time and switch between them.

Subject to the limit of your computer's **RAM**, you can also force the new windows to open yourself, simply by clicking on the Internet Explorer icon again or right-clicking on a link and the selecting the option 'Open in new window'. The Back button will then take you back one step in the narrative, but only in the currently active window. Once the Back button has been used, the Forward button comes into play as a narrative operator, essentially overriding the content of the text using the infrastructure of the software, unless the web designer has disabled the Back button, creating a narrative dead end.

If the window has been spawned by a hyperlink, there is initially no route back – only the options of following another hyperlink, typing a new URL into the address box, or closing the window. Often, when the box is spawned by a hyperlink, it is displayed at a reduced size without browser controls or **toolbars**, so the only option is to close it once you have finished with the content.

A further complication in the narrative machine is created when windows spawn themselves with no input from the user – a pop-up window. At this particular site, the designers have used a pop-up as a pragmatic means of emphasising the importance and currency of the information: a way of signalling that before you use the site, you should know this. All too often, though, pop-ups are used for unsolicited advertising. The content and timing of a pop-up is outside the control of the user. Some will even reappear after they have been closed.

The sense that an already complex and precarious hypertextual narrative has been wrenched from the control of the user, can be deeply disturbing, particularly within the Western post-industrial culture of individualism. We feel individually responsible for the communicative and aesthetic choices we make, and this includes feeling responsible for what is displayed on our computer screens. In an age when we can be prosecuted for the content of the sites that we visit, it is unsettling to be driven to a site without having made the decision to go there yourself. This accounts for the proliferation in recent months of software utilities available for stopping pop-ups altogether. But as Text 9 demonstrates, there are some good pop-ups too.

At the physical centre of Text 9 is the **tagline** for the film: 'A life taken, now Spike and Heaton are running for their own . . .' Graphologically, it is associated with the film title and the Flash animations, but uses a smaller non-italic version of the typeface. It is a convention of film posters to use a smaller font than the title, but, by avoiding the conventional use of a still from the film, or artwork associated with imagery from the film, the page is able to increase the impact of the tagline by centralising it and creating chromatic and typographical connections to other content indicators on the page.

Grammatically, the tagline shows some interesting underlying differences from the noun phrase above it. This time, instead of the need for dense lexical encoding, we see rhetorical devices in action – teasing the audience with intriguing but deliberately partial information. One such device is the **anaphoric reference** from the pronoun 'own' to the noun phrase 'A life', balancing the sentence by placing the concept of life at the beginning and the end, with its significance sufficiently transformed to get our attention so that we want to know more.

Another device worthy of comment is the slightly archaic, high register use of the past participle 'taken' as a post-modifier. The whole noun phrase 'A life taken' then forms a short, rhetorically compressed adverbial phrase that loads the beginning of the sentence with the essence of the film's narrative crisis. We are being invited to end our hypertextual web narrative and step through the looking-glass into a moving image narrative.

NARRATIVE ENFORCEMENT: POP-UP WINDOWS AND SPAM

So far, we have looked only at sites a viewer/reader might *choose* to visit, but our discussion of pop-ups hinted at the idea that new proactive forces on the Web are beginning to encourage a kind of enforced narrative path, where content that we have not chosen may appear on our screens.

Pop-ups are one form of enforced hypertextual narrative, but in recent years another Internet player has muscled in on the Web, issuing invitations to visit websites via one of the oldest manifestations of the Internet – email. Email began life as a text-only medium. Soon after the

Internet explosion of the mid-1990s it developed HTML capability, so that what you could put on a web page you could put in an email and send to a targeted audience.

The problem is that the audience is rarely targeted with any form of market intelligence. It costs virtually nothing to send an email, so the underlying strategy of bulk email marketing is simply to collect email addresses and use them. This unsolicited mail can contain material that most people would seek to avoid, including links to streamed video content. In most cases you are offered a choice about whether to follow the link, but some unsolicited mail contains instructions to spawn pop-up windows. If you are trapped in a hail of pop-up windows, some might say that this is one of the risks of surfing the Web, but to have hyper-text nodes parcelled up and dropped into your Inbox, primed to go off if you go near them, can feel like an invasion of personal space. It is certainly a long way from Tim Berners-Lee's original concept of the Web. At time of writing, one of the best utilities for dealing with this kind of narrative bullying is Spam Inspector, available from http://www.giant-company.com. It does a good job of sniffing out suspect packages and then quarantines them off into a corner, leaving your genuine mail behind. (The origin of the word 'spam' is thought to be the Monty Python sketch featuring a café where everything on the menu was combined with multiple instances of the pressed meat product Spam.)

SUMMARY

At its heart, the Web remains a hypertext-based system for sharing and storing information. The server-browser model is unchanged; but what *has* changed since 1994 is that the browser is routinely capable of handling more *types* of information – most notably audio, video and animation. This unit has been about the linguistic impact of this change: how the narrative pressures of audio and video have in turn put pressure on the Web's linguistic infrastructure. Commercialisation has also brought about the development of more aggressive audience targeting, but our analysis of Text 9 has shown that it is still possible to do this targeting with an intelligent, elegant approach that respects the original aims of the Web and seeks to push it towards new aesthetic frontiers.

1   Do some audience research into which social groups are more likely to view and listen to streamed media via the Web. Do people see the streamed content as the primary reason for visiting the site, or is the use of streamed media more casual and opportunistic? What effect has streamed media had on people's habits in relation to cinema, TV, radio and the purchase of pre-recorded music and video content?

2   Examine the relationship between technology and the use of streamed media via the Web. Is it mainly confined to broadband users? Do people who have upgraded to broadband view the Web in a different way? If streamed media are changing people's perception of the Web, does this mean that the linguistic content of sites is becoming less important?

3   Is it likely that the Web, television, radio and **teletext** will eventually merge into one medium, so that only one device will be needed to experience all electronically transmitted content? Outline the techno-logical and linguistic barriers you think need to be overcome in order for this to happen.

Ready or not: searching the Web

AIMS OF THIS UNIT

Searching is common in most people's experience of the Web. Finding what you want can be very difficult. Nobody maintains the Web as a single store of information: it consists of many interlinked ones. Here, we look at how the language and technology of web searching have come together, and how to apply analytical frameworks to web searches, once we know something about how the technology works.

INDEXES AND CATALOGUES

Libraries and document archives employ skilled people to do two things: find their way around the massive stores of paper-based information; and make a user-friendly guide to where everything is. When people come into the building where the books and documents are stored, they might either browse or go straight to the index to try to find what they want. If it is a paper-based index, it can be organised on cards alphabetically by title, author or subject. There are also systems that put subjects into numerical groups (for example, the Dewey

Decimal system). Each book, box of documents or individual document is labelled with a number or code that enables it to be found from a reference in the index. The books are in neat rows of shelves, and on the end of each row is a label that tells the researcher which books are in that row. Finally, each individual book will have contents pages and probably an index, which help the reader find information within the book. You will still have to do some scanning over pages to get exactly what you want, but the indexing system, which human ingenuity has spent many centuries devising, acts to support you in your search.

Activity

1   Try to find a library or collection of documents that is still indexed using cards in drawers. Some school libraries or smaller collections in university libraries might still be indexed in this way. There might also be older people you know who still have record collections, book collections or collections of rare comics that they have indexed in a similar way.

2   How have the cards been organised? Alphabetically, chronologically or using a special numerical system such as the Dewey Decimal system? Is there a subject index of any kind?

3   Write down the phrase 'the meaning of life'. Use the card index to find out whether the collection of books, documents, records etc. has any information on 'the meaning of life'.

Commentary

You are unlikely to find any book or document titles that contain the whole phrase, 'the meaning of life'. However, you are likely to find some that contain the word 'meaning', and you will almost certainly find several that contain the word 'life'. You will have to make your own decisions about whether to look in the fiction or non-fiction catalogue (if this distinction exists). If there is a subject catalogue, you may find an entry for 'life' but probably not for 'meaning'. There will be no entries in any index or catalogue for 'the' or 'of'. Researching in libraries and archives is based on deciding which lexical words carry the significance of the topic you are researching, and then using the index to locate books, documents, recordings, etc. that relate to your topic. Most of these lexical words will be nouns, often names of people or places. Grammatical words such as determiners and pronouns will need to be stripped out of your phrase before your research begins. Later, when you have gathered information on 'life' and possibly 'meaning', you can start to assess whether you have actually found any useful information on 'the meaning of life'. In other words, it is up to you to put back the significance of the determiner 'the' and the preposition 'of'.

COMPUTERS AS SEARCHERS

Printing, the system that means the written word can be copied and distributed all over the world, is old and well established. Right at the end of this long history, in the second half of the twentieth century, came the computer. In the beginning, computers were like giant calculators, doing numerical tasks only. Later, they could store information as well – customer records, indexes, etc. In the 1960s and 1970s they were huge and expensive, but large companies and organisations could afford to have them and use them for automating processes like billing and record keeping. Libraries began to use them for this purpose in the early 1980s, but to get any information from the index people needed special training, so public readers and researchers still had to rely on paper or microfiche indexes – static printed information that has to be scanned with the eyes.

This was the situation until later in the 1980s, when the **microchip** became cheap and the microcomputer began to be what we know today as the PC: software for searching and changing the records became much easier to use and far less expensive. Terminals for searching indexes began to pop up alongside the paper and microfiche indexes. Suddenly, if the reader could type the word 'fantasy', they could send an automated electronic virtual robot into the records to get a list of everything about fantasy and everything with 'fantasy' in the title (although only the robot could go there, and the reader would have to rely on the robot to bring back the right thing). Once the screen had displayed a list of results from the search, the reader would make a note of the reference numbers for the items they want, and the book or document could be retrieved from the shelf or storeroom.

What if the documents and books were not real though? What if they too were inside the computer? Books and documents are separate bundles of paper. You can pull one off a shelf, but usually they are not stuck together and you don't drag down several books at once. If a book mentions the title of another book, the reader has to look for that other book. If the reader is lucky, it is near where they found the first book, but it is more than likely that they will have to go back to the index and search for the title – in a card index, a microfiche index or a computer index.

What if there were a world where documents were linked to each other from *inside* the document – where the title of another book, mentioned in the text, was also a door that you could open and jump through into that other document or book? This would mean that you could follow a reference *without* going back to the index to search for the next title. This was the vision that Tim Berners-Lee had when he invented the World Wide Web.

Is this a Utopia? In some ways, yes: a web of documents linked with an infinite number of possible paths, enabling instant jumps from one part of the web to another. For example, if a nineteenth-century novel quotes from *King Lear*, when the reader clicks on the quote they jump straight to the right part of the play so they can see exactly where the quote comes from. There may be some difficult or obsolete words in the text, so these words may be highlighted as links, letting the reader jump to definitions of these words. The definition might mention an aspect of Elizabethan culture, and so there might be a link (or doorway) to another document that is devoted to a deeper under-standing of Elizabethan England. Without realising it, the reader will have strayed a long way from the nineteenth-century novel they were reading.

This makes the whole process of reading and research profoundly different from anything experienced in almost the entire history of knowledge, learning and information processing. It is much easier and more intuitive to jump through a ready-made doorway, and arrive at a pre-made destination, than it is to create your own cross-references between documents and keep records of how and why you have made these connections. Also, if you read a paper document again, you might make *different* connections and cross-references with other documents. But web pages have fixed paths, fixed doorways and fixed connections – that always remain open. The process of wandering away from your original document is much more passive and it is therefore easier to lose track of where you started and where you have been.

So, you can travel through massive amounts of accumulated know-ledge without leaving your house. But it is not like a library. This is how the word 'surf' came to be used for the experience of looking at web pages: it is almost as if you are being carried by forces that you don't control. If you go to a library and just sit in a chair, nothing will happen, but with the minimal effort of clicking a mouse you can very quickly be surrounded by information – metaphorically lost at sea.

This is where search engines come in. They offer you a way of finding what you want on the Web. Given that pages are being added to the Web at a rate of hundreds per minute, how do the search engines keep track of what is out there? The answer is that they use a software agent called a 'spider', which never-endingly crawls over the Web and tells the search engine about the pages it finds. The search engine keeps its own index of key words from as many pages as it can find, and this index is constantly being updated.

To see this in action, go to http://gigablast.com (see Text 10: Gigablast) and look at the figure in the middle of the page, which tells you how many pages this search engine has indexed. If you click on the Refresh button at the top of your browser window, you will see the number increase. Even if you only wait a few seconds before clicking it again, you will notice that the number goes up by several hundred.

Text 10: Gigablast

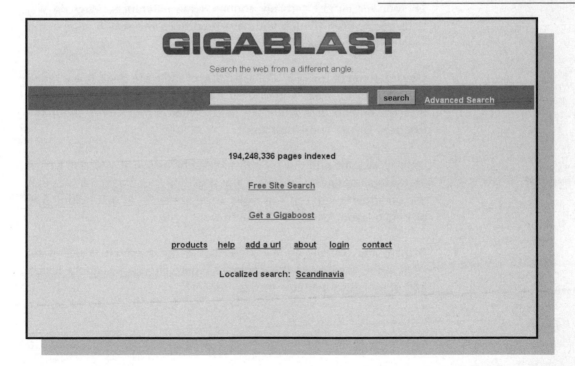

GIGABLAST

Search the web from a different angle.

search   Advanced Search

194,248,336 pages indexed

Free Site Search

Get a Gigaboost

products   help   add a url   about   login   contact

Localized search: Scandinavia

Activity

1   Try another research exercise, this time using the Internet. If you go to http://altavista.com you will be presented with a box near the top of the page, asking you what you want to search for. This is called a simple search or simple query and most search engines will offer you this by default.

2   Type in the phrase 'the meaning of life' and click on Search, or press Enter/Return. Wait for the results to load, and then print out that page (only the first page), preferably in colour.

3   Which words have been highlighted in the list of hits? How have the lexical and grammatical words in the search phrase ('the meaning of life') been handled differently?

4   How is each hit presented? Which part of the page is given to you? Which part(s) of the hit are presented as hyperlinks?

5   There is an example of the same query reproduced below. Your own printout will almost certainly contain some differences. Why do you think this is, even though you have used the same search engine and exactly the same query?

6   Click on some of the hits, and see if any of them are **dead links**. When the link is dead, what kind of error messages do you get? Why would a search engine give you dead links? What is interesting about the language of the error messages?

7   Looking at your printout (or the screenshot below, if you don't have access to a computer), are there any structural (discourse) features that you find interesting; can you make any comments on graphology (use of fonts), layout or use of colour?

8   Is there any content on the page that is not a search result? If so, what is the purpose of this content? What can you say about lexical and grammatical patterns in this content?

Text 11: altavista

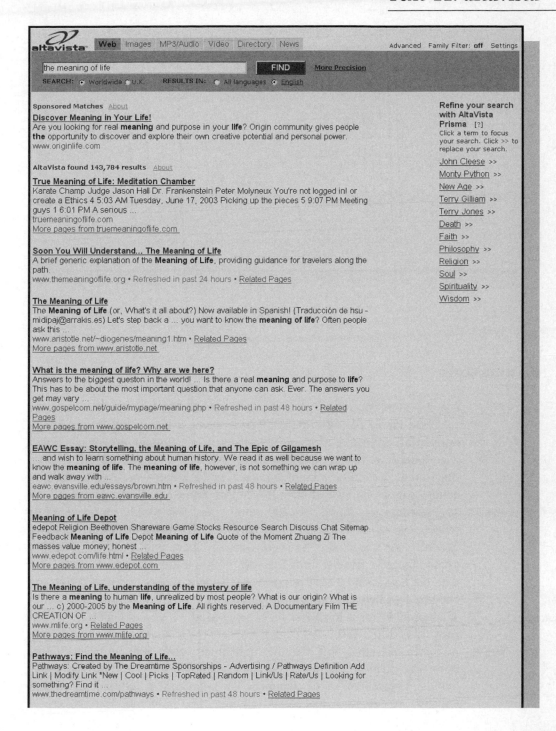

FAQ about the Meaning of Life
Real, non-cryptic, intelligent, satisfying answers you haven't heard. Our place in the cosmos,
our ... can come from?2.5: What is the **Meaning of Life**?3: Miscellaneous.3.1: What's this
business ...
www.sysopmind.com/tmol-faq/meaningoflife.html • Refreshed in past 48 hours • Related
Pages
More pages from www.sysopmind.com

Meet ron218 @ AmericanSingles.com - (Keywords: Indiana, the meaning of life...,
Oldies , Actor)
... ron218 @ AmericanSingles.com - (Keywords: Indiana, the **meaning of life**..., Oldies ,
Actor) Actor, Artist, Builder A diamond in the ... ron218 Indiana, the **meaning of life**...,
Oldies , American ...
www.americansingles.com/default.asp?p=70...86301&prm=17002
More pages from www.americansingles.com

Extend your Search: About
Search for Local Websites about **the meaning of life** at WebFinder.com
Search for **the meaning of life** on eBay.co.uk

Result Pages: 1 2 3 4 5 6 7 8 9 10 [Next >>]   Back To Top

Business Services   Submit a Site   Advertise   About AltaVista   Help

© 2003 AltaVista

Commentary

For the searcher, the most important part of the page is the sentence
'AltaVista found 143,784 results'. This sentence is interesting from a **sociolinguistic** perspective, because it is written in Standard American English
even though we are on the UK version of the site. In Standard British English,
the simple past tense cannot be used to describe a recently completed
action: you would instead have to use the primary auxiliary 'has/have' and
say 'AltaVista has found 143,784 results'. So, this simple sentence subtly
reflects the American dominance of the Web. Along with the sentence
'Extend your search' and the noun phrase 'Sponsored Matches', it is also
graphologically isolated from the rest of the page through the use of a
different colour and a smaller point size. Where a website is interactive and
choices are offered about the next action the user would like to perform,
it is common for a hyperlink to be expressed as an instruction using the
root form of the verb – 'extend'.

You will often find that the highlighted words are the lexical words
from your query – 'meaning' and 'life'. Grammatical words (such as determiners, prepositions and conjunctions) tend to be ignored by search
engines. In this way, the search engine tries to imitate the process of

researching in a library – by dividing up your search into two lexically significant topic areas ('meaning' and 'life').

However, the search engine seems to have the sense that 'the meaning of life' is a very frequently used phrase, as indicated by the number of hits produced by the search – 143,784. Whether the search engine software *knows* that the phrase is **idiomatic**, and tries to prioritise hits that use the phrase in a way that relates to the cultural significance of the phrase and hence its pragmatic force rather than just its lexical **sense**, is a key question in the development of search engine software. The hyperlinks immediately below the query box, and to the right of the list of hits, seem to suggest this semantic capability. Like the query phrase itself, these hyperlinks are noun phrases – but they have no lexical relation to the search phrase, only semantic relations. The search engine has specifically picked up on some purely semantic relations:

◎   the fact that *The Meaning of Life* was a Monty Python film and people such as John Cleese starred in it;

◎   the fact that the film *The Meaning Of Life* was a comedy;

◎   the fact that 'life' is an **antonym** of 'death';

◎   the assumption that religion helps people look for meaning in life;

◎   the cliché that philosophy does the same thing from a more secular perspective;

◎   the idea that life is perceived through the senses;

◎   the fact that the noun 'spirituality' has a **synonymous** relationship with the noun 'religion'.

Each hit gives you the **title** of the page, followed by the first few lines of text from that page, followed by the URL of the page. To get to the page represented by each hit, you can click on *either* the title *or* the URL. This is a form of built-in **exophoric reference** common to most web pages – a set of hard-wired gateways to other documents. Search engine hits are a more extreme version of this type of exophoric reference, because they are really *only* of any value in relation to the external documents to which they are linked.

A page of search engine hits has many complex structural features, and is very far from the simple page of HTML, with basic hyperlinks, that we discussed in Unit one (pp. 7–20). A search engine's primary function is to refer *outside* of itself – an extreme example of exophoric reference; but there are also some important structural features *within* the page – features that contribute towards the house style of search engine results pages.

It is customary to replicate the search dialogue, containing the phrase that the user has typed, at the top or the bottom of the page. This establishes lexical cohesion between the search phrase and the hits. The more times the key lexical words appear in the hit, the stronger is the cohesive bond and the more likely the hit is to appear near the top of the list.

There is a relationship between the number of hits and the perceived success of the search. The pragmatic effect of results in the hundreds of thousands is that the searcher will conclude the search has been unsuccessful or the search query needs to be refined for the information to become usable. Even though it is physically impossible to browse through 143,784 pages, it remains a convention of search engines that all the possibilities are presented to the user near the top of the page and that there is a visual link between that number and a set of hyperlinks near the bottom. Within that set of hyperlinks, all of the hits are parcelled up into batches of ten. Making this connection between the two areas of the page relies on the user scrolling to the bottom of the page and scanning downwards to register the lexically cohesive repetition of the lexeme 'result'.

The repetition of the AltaVista logo is an aspect of corporate branding. The logo consists of lower-case sans serif text and a stylised lower-case letter 'a' in symbol form – graphologically signalling unique identity and relevance in a technological world.

A search engine performs a typographical transformation. It takes the content of several sites and displays them in its own standardised font, thus layering its own house style over them. Notice that none of the graphical elements of the sites appear in the search engine's results list – the focus of the search being the textual content of the website you are looking for. Many modern search engines now present you with different types of search, so that if you are looking for images, video or audio files these pre-refined searches can be found in a separate section of the site. In the AltaVista example, there are hyperlinks to these sections above the main query box. An interesting feature here is that these hyperlinks are presented like tabs on a card index – a feature that appears not only on websites but in much computer software, drawing on the cultural assumption that a computer environment is more user-friendly if it somehow mimics a paper document. As we have discovered repeatedly in this book, though, the experience of browsing the Web is very different from absorbing information from paper sources.

Most search engines will describe the outcome of your search in terms of 'results' or '**matches**'. Again, the relationship between these two words is a semantic one of synonymy: they are not lexically related. This search engine uses both terms, but there is a subtle pragmatic difference between them. The word 'matches' is **pre-modified** by 'sponsored'. Combined with the use of a different noun, this pre-modification sets up the assumption that sponsored matches are not quite the same as results. Results are the whole bag – everything that the engine has found, but sponsored matches are given higher priority through their placement on the page and the implication that these sites are being promoted as part of a financial agreement.

THE LANGUAGE OF DEAD LINKS

As we illustrated earlier by repeatedly refreshing the Gigablast page (p. 71), the Web is constantly changing. New pages are being added every second, but pages are also being constantly removed. The search engine's web spider will find new pages and index them, but if a page is deleted the spider will not know until it visits that site again – so the URL remains in the index and a dead link is the result. The most common message to appear when you follow a dead link is 'Error 404 – Page Not Found'. This is a code generated by a web server when it is asked for a page that it does not have. It is such a common occurrence when web browsing, that the term '**404**' is starting to be used in everyday life as a metaphor for a person who is clueless or generally unaware. For example, 'Don't bother asking him. He's 404, man.'

Another common error message starts with 'The page cannot be displayed'. Unlike the simpler 404 error, this page comes from your own computer and is usually a sign that there is something temporarily wrong with your Internet connection. If you look at Text 12: This Page Cannot Be Displayed, you will see that the opening sentence is a forbidding one. As we saw in the Unit one (pp. 7–20), some of the earliest incarnations of web pages used black text on a plain white background with very little graphical content. The pragmatic effect of this now is to signal a very functional page, which provides a combination of information and advice. The relative absence of graphical content is in itself a marker of formality. Messages like this are specific to the software environment that the user is working in – so, in a very real sense, it is a message from Microsoft.

Apart from the lack of graphical content, there are a number of linguistic strategies used to indicate that the supposed error is outside Microsoft's control and may very well require technical intervention. For example, the use of the negative, **passive** verb phrase 'The page cannot be displayed' in the opening sentence is a grammatical way of reinforcing the suggestion that the software has tried its best to display the page but that this is impossible for reasons outside its control. Key **modal verbs** in the opening paragraph then set up some very general possibilities for the cause of the problem: someone needs to sort out a technical fault, but the software is not sure who. The arrangement of the following paragraphs as bullet points signals a degree of formality but also indicates that none of the suggested steps have priority over each other. There is a repeated use of **conditional** clauses (introduced by the **relativiser** 'if') to reinforce the assumption that different possible circumstances require different avenues of investigation.

Text 12 is transactional in a way that is almost unique to web pages, because it contains hyperlinks to other web pages (the Back button) and also hyperlinks to configuration settings for the user's computer.

Text 13: These Weapons of Mass Destruction Cannot Be Displayed, is a parody of the all too familiar error page, which refers to the situation in Iraq immediately after the 2003 Gulf War. The reason given by Britain and America, for going to war, was to halt the development of Iraq's weapons of mass destruction programme. Weapons inspectors from the United Nations had already been performing this task for several years, since the first Gulf War in 1991, but the patience of Britain and America finally ran out in 2003, leading to a full-scale ground invasion of the country – an invasion about which many governments had misgivings. It is also fair to say that public opinion in Britain and the US was not fully behind the action – especially in Britain. The problem faced by the allies in the aftermath of the war was that the most determined scouring of suspect sites throughout Iraq was unable to uncover any evidence of weapons of mass destruction having been developed or manufactured during at least the last decade.

If you look at this satirical version of the error page taken from http://www.coxar.pwp.blueyonder.co.uk and printed here following the real one, you will see that the wording and structure of the original have been echoed very precisely. For the humour to work, the graphological, lexical and graphical content of the page need to spark instant recognition. Careful attention has been paid to replicating the icons, font and layout of the original. A brief test on a sample audience will quickly reveal that the humour does work – so we conclude the page is a frequently experienced one which contributes to the still widely held view that browsing and searching the Web can be a frustrating process for largely technical reasons.

As we discussed in Unit four (pp. 53–65), users maintain a level of tolerance for technical errors when browsing or searching the Web – a much higher level than they would allow when, for example, watching television. If you received a message telling you that TV channels or programmes could not be displayed for unexplained technical reasons, you would quite quickly conclude that you were paying for a service that was inherently unreliable, and you would complain. No single body governs or is responsible for the content of the Web. There is no one to complain to, so we put up with it. Anthony Coxar's satirical version of the Internet Explorer error page very cleverly taps into its familiarity as a symbol of the Web experience – using the grammatical and graphological framework as a template for expressing a political viewpoint.

COMPARING SEARCH ENGINES

Just as two people would be unlikely to index a collection of documents in precisely the same way, or to use the index in the same way, two search engines will handle the same query differently. One very common difference will be the raw number of hits produced from the same search string. This comes from the fact that spiders for different search engines operate in different ways and at different times, so that the different indexes of pages will not contain the same URLs. Also the search software will query the index in a way that is as individual as the person or people who wrote the software.

Some search engines operate a system called **page caching** in which copies of indexed pages are stored on the search engine server for faster access, so that you do not have to connect to another site to see the page. Where the pages offered by the list of hits have been **cached**, this will be clearly indicated for each individual hit.

Another common way of arranging hits is something called **site clustering**. This is where the search engine will try to avoid listing multiple pages from the same site, so as not to clutter the list; where a second page from the same site appears in the list, it is displayed immediately underneath the main page and indented. Most search engines now operate site clustering.

Text 12: The Page Cannot Be Displayed

> ### ℹ The page cannot be displayed
>
> The page you are looking for is currently unavailable. The Web site might be experiencing technical difficulties, or you may need to adjust your browser settings.
>
> ---
>
> Please try the following:
>
> - Click the ⟳ Refresh button, or try again later.
> - If you typed the page address in the Address bar, make sure that it is spelled correctly.
> - To check your connection settings, click the **Tools** menu, and then click **Internet Options**. On the **Connections** tab, click **Settings**. The settings should match those provided by your local area network (LAN) administrator or Internet service provider (ISP).
> - If your Network Administrator has enabled it, Microsoft Windows can examine your network and automatically discover network connection settings.
>   If you would like Windows to try and discover them,
>   click 🔍 Detect Network Settings
> - Some sites require 128-bit connection security. Click the **Help** menu and then click **About Internet Explorer** to determine what strength security you have installed.
> - If you are trying to reach a secure site, make sure your Security settings can support it. Click the **Tools** menu, and then click **Internet Options**. On the Advanced tab, scroll to the Security section and check settings for SSL 2.0, SSL 3.0, TLS 1.0, PCT 1.0.
> - Click the ⇐ Back button to try another link.
>
> Cannot find server or DNS Error
> Internet Explorer

Text 13: These Weapons of Mass Destruction Cannot Be Displayed

[i] These Weapons of Mass Destruction cannot be displayed

The weapons you are looking for are currently unavailable. The country might be experiencing technical difficulties, or you may need to adjust your weapons inspectors mandate.

Please try the following:

- Click the [*] Regime change button, or try again later.
- If you are George Bush and typed the country's name in the address bar, make sure that it is spelled correctly. (IRAQ).
- To check your weapons inspector settings, click the **UN** menu, and then click **Weapons Inspector Options**. On the **Security Council** tab, click **Consensus**. The settings should match those provided by your government or NATO.
- If the Security Council has enabled it, The United States of America can examine your country and automatically discover Weapons of Mass Destruction.
  If you would like to use the CIA to try and discover them,
  click [⊙] Detect weapons
- Some countries require 128 thousand troops to liberate them. Click the **Panic** menu and then click **About US foreign policy** to determine what regime they will install.
- If you are an Old European Country trying to protect your interests, make sure your options are left wide open as long as possible. Click the **Tools** menu, and then click on **League of Nations**. On the Advanced tab, scroll to the Head in the Sand section and check settings for your exports to Iraq.
- Click the [✦] Bomb button if you are Donald Rumsfeld.

Cannot find weapons or CIA Error
Iraqi Explorer

Activity

1   Go to http://gigablast.com and enter the same search phrase that you used in the last activity – the meaning of life. (It is important not to use speech marks.) Click on the 'blast it!' (search) button and then print out the resulting page, as you did for the AltaVista search.

2   Place the two printouts alongside each other (or compare Texts 12 and 14), and see if you can find any overall differences of layout, colour, graphology, discourse structure, grammar, lexis, semantics or pragmatic meaning.

3   You will see that many of the hits are the same; but are the same hits presented in a different way by Gigablast?

4   Are there any linguistic clues that might suggest the two search engines are run and maintained by different types of organisation?

Text 14: Gigablast Search Results

GIGABLAST | the meaning of life | blast it!

Results 1 to 10 of about 2,301,706. The following query words were ignored: **the of**. Preceed each with a '+' or wrap in quotes to not ignore.

The Meaning of Life
...get those people back on track with some "pre-**meaning of life**" advice: If you're questioning **the meaning of life**.....may be ready for the next step in this exposition on **the meaning of life**. Of course, if you're like most people, you.....back a moment.. Why do you want to know **the meaning of life**? Often people ask this question when they really want..
www.anstotle.net/~diogenes/meaning1.htm - 2.5k - [cached] - indexed: May 25 2002 - modified: Jul 08 2000

True Meaning of Life: Meditation Chamber
...for entertainment and does not represent the views of the persons/characters portrayed within.....Feiss.. 5.. 2:49 PM.. Sunday, June 15, 2003.. Here comes the sun.. 2.. 11:44 PM.. The Secret.. 3.. 3:34 PM.. Tron.. 2.....15.. 12:17 AM.. Thursday, June 5, 2003.. Value of education.. 6.. 1:00 PM.. Re: Samurai Kenshin? 2.. 6:36..
www.truemeaningoflife.com - 19.7k - [cached] - indexed: Jun 16 2003

The Meaning of Life--A Spiritual Book by Tom Gregory--Now Available at...
...of whimsy, Tom Gregory shows us not only how to infuse **life** with **meaning**, but how to create a better world. " - Ben.....and help people change their lives."   **The Meaning of Life**.. TABLE OF CONTENTS.. Introduction.. My Search for.....Click for info.. Tom Gregory, the author of **The Meaning of Life**, is a new voice in the field of..
www.meaningoflife.net - 30.7k - [cached] - indexed: Nov 11 2002 - modified: Jul 07 2002

Monty Python's The Meaning of Life (1983)
...submit a comment.. Celeb Photos.. More! Monty Python's **The Meaning of Life** (1983) Page 1 of 31.. Directed by.. Terry.....Monty Python's **The Meaning of Life** (1983) - Cast, Crew, Reviews, Plot Summary.....15 June 2000..Summary: Weird, bizarre and wonderful.. **The Meaning of Life** is usual Monty Pythons-stuff. This time they..
us.imdb.com/Title?0085959 - 47.6k - [cached] - indexed: Jun 26 2003

FAQ about the Meaning of Life
...changed my **life**. I'm satisfied this is the real **Meaning of Life**. I'm glad I read this page. I don't believe a word of.....2: Logic.2.1: What is the problem of asking "What is **the meaning of life**?"2.2: What are choices? What are goals?2.3.....will happen to the human race? 3.5: Isn't "happiness" **the meaning of life**?3.6: How can I become a better person?3.7..
www.sysopmind.com/tmol-faq/meaningoflife.html - 13.9k - [cached] - indexed: May 24 2002 - modified: Oct 10 2000

The Meaning of Life
...a life of meaning?....The Meaning of Life.. - A Life of Meaning.. The Meaning of Life: An Ageless Search.. What is.....significance. The Meaning of Life? To live a life of meaning! Who is God? God.. Meaning of Life.. Free Will.....for the meaning of your life has begun. The Meaning of Life: How to fulfill your Mission.. The challenge to the..
www.the-meaning-of--life.com - 17.3k - [cached] - indexed: Dec 28 2002 - modified: Jul 28 2002

What is the meaning of life?
...to the "meaning of life", see: The Net's Meaning of Life .Meaning of Life submissions ..the meaning of life in the.....is to increase fitness....What is the meaning of life? The meaning of life is to increase fitness.. This is the quick....Meaning of Life, Comment by Chante Hall..The meaning of life, Comment by David Knowles..what is life?, Comment by..
pespmc1.vub.ac.be/MEANLIFE.html - 15.7k - [cached] - indexed: Aug 19 2002 - modified: Aug 07 2002

The Meaning of Life, understanding of the mystery of life
...click to continue..   • Life.. • The Meaning of Life? • Creation or Evolution? • Destiny.. • By itself.....it seems, fails to understand that purpose. The Meaning of Life will help you to understand the mystery of life. This.....TOUCH here... Copyright(c) 2000-2005 by the Meaning of Life. All rights reserved.   A Documentary Film..
www.mlife.org - 27.8k - [cached] - indexed: Jan 27 2003 - modified: Sep 26 2002

The Robinson Homestead
...13Belgians.. Other Critters?: 3 old hens.. The Meaning of Life?: living life to the fullest ,in harmaney with nature.....four goats,one wether.one mini pig.. The Meaning of Life?: Living life one day at a time doing the best youcan.....four goats,one wether.one mini pig.. The Meaning of Life?: Living life one day at a time doing the best youcan..
www.geocities.com/Heartland/Pointe/1915/geobook.html - 67.0k - [cached] - indexed: Jun 11 2002 - modified: Jun 11 2002

THE NET'S MEANING OF LIFE
...s Life"Night Panthers .Night Panthers.. "We have to find life´s meaning for one reason: it doesn´t have a meaning....life" Douglas Adams..Dave Levy.. "A twinkies' Meaning of Life is to be enjoyed like the stupid snack cake that...mmm.....forever."Kelley Essoe..Kelley Essoe.. "The meaning of life is to do God's Will."Kurt Welton..Kurt Welton.. "Take..
www.geocities.com/Broadway/2230/mlife.html - 7.7k - [cached] - indexed: Aug 18 2002 - modified: Oct 25 1996
[More results from this site]

Next 10 Results

Try your search on   google   yahoo   alltheweb   alta vista   teoma   wisenut

Commentary

The first point to notice is that the raw number of hits is very different. This indicates a profound difference in the way the search engine software has handled the lexical, grammatical and semantic relations suggested by your search query. Precisely how the software does this is more within the realm of computer programming and **artificial intelligence** and is outside the scope of this book – but it would make a very interesting language investigation topic for someone who also had a background in computer programming.

The use of the phrase 'refreshed in the past 48 hours' on the AltaVista page is interesting lexically. The word 'refresh' within the semantic field of web browsing has come to mean the process of reloading the page by clicking on the Refresh button at the top of the browser window – which you can demonstrate easily by going to http://news.bbc.co.uk and then leaving that browser window displayed for several hours before clicking the Refresh button. The content will change as the headline news moves on.

Playing on this association, common to most people's browsing experience, the phrase 'refreshed in the past 48 hours' indicates how recently the index has updated its information about the content of the page.

Gigablast conveys this information by breaking the concept down into two separate processes: instead of the single past participle 'refreshed' we have two – 'indexed' and 'modified'. Past participles are often used in English to indicate completed actions in the recent past: with Gigablast, we are told when the spider first indexed the document and also when it updated its record of that document.

The layout and use of graphology are remarkably similar, with AltaVista perhaps using slightly more colour and graphical content. This perhaps suggests a standardised format for search engine results that may be driven by more general trends in web page design.

ADVANCED SEARCHING AND BOOLEAN LOGIC

Most people's experience of trying to find things on the Internet comes from experimenting with different words or phrases at the default page for their favourite search engine. It is easy to go to http://google.com and just experiment until you get the information you want. Indeed, this is now such a widespread way of searching that the term 'Googling' is starting to become synonymous with web searching. Almost all search engines, including Google, do however have an advanced searching section, which is based primarily on a computer programming principle called **Boolean logic**. This borrows a few words from natural human language and gives them precise logical value.

As most modern linguists will tell you, human language does not work in an entirely logical way. Otherwise, there would be, for example, no irregular verbs in any language. But computers are, despite myths propagated by science fiction stories, much less intelligent and adaptable than humans – so they need absolute logic and precision in the instructions they are given.

In this context the conjunction 'AND' and the preposition 'NEAR' are most important. If you want pages related to a specific Harold Pinter play, you could enter the search query: 'Pinter' AND 'The Homecoming'. This would *only* include in its results pages with *exactly* the words or phrases in quote marks. The quote marks tell the software to treat the characters between them as a complete, unbreakable phrase, which must appear on the page in that form. All other pages would be excluded from the search. The operator 'NEAR' can narrow searches even further, so that the two phrases must appear within about ten words of each other.

Go to http://uk.altavista.com/help/adv_search/syntax for a more comprehensive explanation of some terms that can be used to narrow web searches.

SUMMARY

This unit is not intended to give the impression that web searching is a replacement for using libraries or document archives. Rather, it attempts, from a linguistic perspective, to look at some of the angst produced when a researcher realises that the Web contains vast amounts of information which will take a great deal of sifting and refining to be of any use – and certainly if it is going to be of any *academic* value.

The sense that you are lost at sea, and surrounded by more data than you can deal with, is a common one and has led many to reject the Web as a tool for serious research. A library is a highly focused, self-censoring environment, whereas the Web grows without censorship and without overall organisation of content. Like Neo in *The Matrix* we need software agents to help us find what we need – but if we can only remember the kind of language the agents understand, the Holy Grail is definitely out there.

Extension

1   Visit any web page, and then select the menu option View, sub-menu option Source in your browser window. This should pop up a window with the HTML source code of the page and near the top you should see the phrase '<META NAME="Keywords" content="'. Following this are all the hidden keywords that the site owners want search engine spiders to include in their index. Explore the semantic and lexical relationships between the keywords and the site content. Do the keywords

85

unveil a hidden agenda essentially outside the explicit lexical frame-work of the site?

2　　Experiment with some of the analytical tools used in this unit, but try them out on search engines other than AltaVista and Gigablast: Google and Lycos, for example. Do you think the linguistic patterns are similar?

3　　Use some of the analytical tools from this unit to make similar obser-vations about the advanced searching facilities offered by various search engines. How does the language of advanced web searching differ from the natural human language that you might use if you went into a library and presented a similar query to a librarian?

The raw materials of web writing

Web pages make their methods of construction available for anyone to look at, in a way that no other type of communication does. What difference does this make to us as analysers of web text? Does availability of the blueprints for the web page help us to analyse it?

TWO LANGUAGES OF THE WEB

When we talk about the language of websites, we need to recognise that language on the Web has two basic flavours. The linguistic analysis in this book has necessarily concentrated most on natural human language, as used by people. The Intertext series looks at aspects of how language works in different social contexts, and how these contexts generate unique language varieties. In this sense, the Web is no different from newspapers, comics, sport, advertising or any of the other titles in the series. It is a mass medium through which people express themselves linguistically.

But there is another language of websites – HTML. Its special codes are hidden from the viewer/reader of the web page, in the same way as the technology of printing is hidden from a newspaper reader. However, the unique quality of website publishing comes from the fact that the technology of its publishing is not buried very deeply. As we saw in Unit five (pp. 67–86), two clicks of a mouse will show you the source code. This level of democratisation, whereby the end user is given direct access to the means of production, would be unknown in any other medium. It would be rather like attaching to each copy of a newspaper a computer disk containing all the **desktop publishing** files and picture files that had been used to create the edition of the paper, thus giving some insight into the design process. By contrast, the covert language of websites – the underlying code – can easily be seen by peeling away a very thin top layer.

Is a knowledge of HTML necessary to write web pages? Certainly, a newspaper reporter only really needs to know how to type text into a terminal. It is the job of the sub-editors, typesetters and graphic artists to finalise page design and layout. A similar process operates with professional, institutional websites: the typed copy is sent to the design team who add the appropriate HTML **tags** and publish the finished text in the typographical house style of the site, selecting the area of the page layout where the text will appear. However, amateur web publishers do not have teams of specialists at their disposal. So how exactly do they do it?

WHAT YOU SEE IS *NOT* WHAT YOU GET

The Web is fundamentally just **plain text**. In the early days, when the novelty lay in the sharing and structuring of information using hypertextual pathways, and the appearance of an image here and there was an added decorative bonus, all websites were built using **text editors**. The most well-known text editor is Notepad – a utility that has shipped with Microsoft Windows since its inception in 1985. It cannot handle fonts or bold or underlining and you cannot put pictures into it: it handles **characters** generated by a standard keyboard, and nothing else. To this day, professional web designers do a significant proportion of their work using a text editor. Peeling back the formatting added by the web browser, a simple layout would look something like the example on p. 89: an extract from Text 1 in Unit one (pp. 7–20).

Scanning quickly through this example, it is not difficult to identify large chunks of human language. If you just type text into Notepad, and save the file with the HTM or HTML **file extension** after the dot, a web browser will be able to open the file and display the text in the

```
<p>
<li><A href="/htmlContent.jhtml?html=/archive/1996/06/05/nyob105.html">
Grinning suspect sees wake-up call as a compliment</A></li><p>
<p><!— start summary —>POLICE in London and Manchester yesterday
arrested eight men suspected of involvement in <A href="/htmlContent.jhtml?
html=/archive/science/1996/03/25/fsara23.html">football hooliganism</A>
in dawn operations designed to deter those intent on causing trouble at the
Euro 96 tournament.<!— end summary —><p>
The operations also <A href="/htmlContent.jhtml?html=/archive/1996/05/01/
ntik01.html">cast doubt on the efficacy of the ticketing system</A> after one
of the men was found to have 12 tickets he obtained in his own name.<p>
Four Tottenham Hotspur supporters and two Arsenal fans were arrested in the
raids, which started at 5am, at a series of houses across north London and
Essex. A seventh man walked into Highgate police station later in the day and
was arrested.<p>
Greater Manchester police arrested one man after they visited eight homes in an
operation against suspected hooligans. In a separate operation, Manchester
officers <A href="/htmlContent.jhtml?html=/archive/1996/02/26/nsuic225.
html">investigating the activities of the far-Right group Combat 18</A>
arrested three men and seized documents and videos.<p>
In London, Operation Take-Off, involving more than 70 officers and four
dog-handlers, recovered the Euro 96 tickets, a sword, a bayonet and three
knives.<p>
Five adults and a juvenile were charged last night with violent disorder.<p>
Police moved after studying video film of a fight at the <A href="/html
Content.jhtml?html=/archive/1996/04/16/sfguna16.html">Arsenal-Spurs
game at Highbury in April</A> which involved 30 to 40 hooligans attempting
to reach each other through a thinly-defended cordon of police officers and
stewards.<p>
Seats and punches were thrown and a policeman was knocked unconscious.
It seems that by inviting the media to witness the raids, the Metropolitan Police
was keen to make clear its intentions with the European Championship due to
start on Saturday.<p>
<h4> The man arrested yesterday had four tickets for England's opening game
with Switzerland and four for the following weekend's clash with
Scotland</h4><p>
```

default system font. But, however many times you have pressed the Return key in Notepad, the web browser will not display these as paragraph breaks. Every aspect of the layout has to be **coded**. Each element of the text appearing inside pointed brackets < > will be hidden from the display and treated as instructions to the browser. These are known as 'tags'. A simple example is the tag <p>, which instructs the browser to display a paragraph break. Some tags need to be turned on and then turned off again. The last paragraph of the text above appears in the browser as bold text. This is achieved by switching on heading style number 4 with instruction <h4> and then switching it off at the end of the paragraph with the tag </h4>. The forward slash character before a tag always indicates that the instruction is to be switched off. If it were not switched off, the whole of the rest of the page would appear in bold.

As we implied in Unit four when looking at the digital revolution of the 1980s, computers have no imagination (p. 54). To adapt a quote from the first *Terminator* movie, you cannot bargain with them, or plead with them; they do not feel pity, or remorse or fear, and they absolutely will not stop until they are told to in the right way. If a computer appears to understand natural language, it is because it has been programmed with some very sophisticated instructions, which tell it to respond in specific ways according to the data it has received. The same context, and the same data, will always produce the same response. Humans are less reliable.

When your computer freezes and loses you the assignment (due in the next day) that you have spent the last few hours typing, it is being entirely predictable – but the interaction between machine and software is so complex that the contextual factors are too many for anyone to know fully: therefore, the computer *appears* to be unpredictable. But it is not personal, however much it might seem that way.

Now, what if there were a magical device, like a word processor, that would take care of the tags for you, hide them away, and just let you concentrate on typing and formatting the text as if you were using a word processor?

Activity

The dream comes true with the advent of WYSIWYG (What You See Is What You Get) HTML editing software, and it is apt that one of the most powerful HTML editors around today is called Dreamweaver. Raw HTML coding rests securely within the tradition of computer programming. Programmers have to check the logic of their instructions to the computer, and HTML coders have to check the logic of their tags, but a WYSIWYG editor will allow you to operate purely on text and layout, generating the tags for you automatically.

Text 15: HTML Source Code, and Text 16: HTML Displayed, are screenshots from a **Freeware** HTML editor called Matizha, available at http://www. matizha.com/en/. The screenshots show the **Edit View** and the **Design View** of the same web page.

1   Is it possible to use traditional textual analysis frameworks to make a comparison of Text 15 and Text 16; or is Text 15 irrelevant within the study of natural human language?

2   Can you think of any *linguistic* reasons why we still need to see the code when we are designing web pages? Why have HTML editors not gone the way of word processors and completely covered up the coding process?

Text 15: HTML Source Code

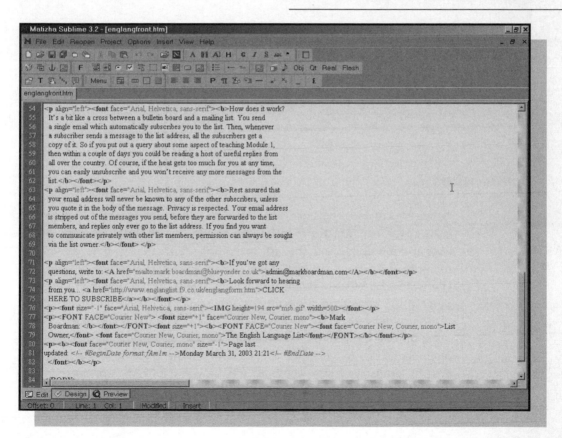

Text 16: HTML Displayed

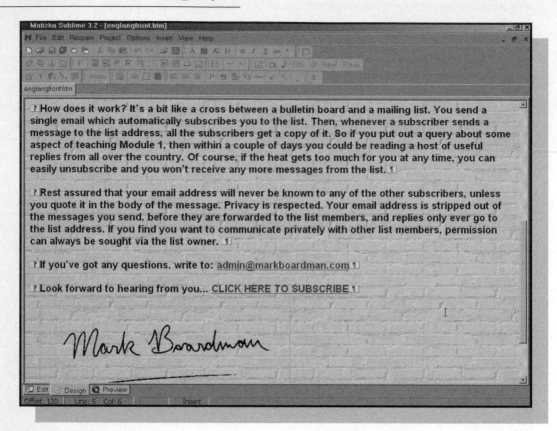

Commentary

When we create web pages, are we writers or are we coders? The answer is that we are both. Experienced site designers still prefer to work at the level of raw code, and the act of coding at the same time as writing the natural language content of websites is unique as a communicative act. The writer-coder has to maintain the unforgiving, logical syntax of the computer at the same time as monitoring the infinite pragmatic possibilities that can be generated by the forms and functions of human language.

On one level, HTML code can be seen as a highly sophisticated form of punctuation. As you type the content of the page, you interrupt the flow of letters with instructions to the browser. Indeed, it is open to the same kind of flexible application as traditional punctuation. It is definitely true that in many cases there will be more than one way of coding the same effect, and coders do speak of 'elegance' in the use of tags. Some methods are more efficient than others, and inefficient coding of large pages can mean that they will load more slowly.

Text 15 is a transitional text – a response to the context of composition, production and preparation for publishing – the electronic equivalent of operating the now obsolete **Linotype** machine.

It is possible to type the content and use word-processor style formatting actions in Design View, but many find it comforting to see the raw code. Depending on your level of coding expertise, Text 15 and Text 16 can swap roles, according to whether we see ourselves as creating for the idiosyncrasies of the computer or for the human viewers/readers who will respond to the page as a cultural artefact.

Returning to the concept of bricolage that we looked at in Unit three (pp. 37–51), any web designer will tell you that no WYSIWYG editor on the planet can fulfil *all* possible design briefs without the need to resort to code at least occasionally. For this reason, it is common practice to collect snippets of code that are known to perform useful tasks. Amateur designers often do not know fully how these snippets of code work, and could not reproduce them if they were lost. Rather, they are collected and combined at **macro** level using a half-understood syntax based on a combination of observation and intuition: even if you habitually use Design View, you will have to switch back into the unforgiving world of raw computer instruction, and paste the code into the Edit View window in exactly the right place.

Now that the original HTML concept has been supplemented by two powerful programming languages, Java and JavaScript, a lot can be lost in translation when a WYSIWYG editor tries to predict what the coded whole will look like in the browser. Because of the inherent unreliability of WYSIWYG editors, the practice of code snippet bricolage persists in maintaining the illusion that we are all potentially expert coders – collecting, customising, living life on the edge.

SUMMARY: FULL CIRCLE

> And the end of all our searching shall be to return to the place where we started and know it for the first time.
>
> (T.S. Eliot)

An oral tradition of textual transmission relies on human memory. In some oral cultures, linguistic art forms such as poetry are partially extemporised by building them out of known formulaic elements: a practice along these lines persisted in Anglo-Saxon narrative poetry. The original context of production was oral, but we know about it now, in spite of the death of the culture and the language, because the artefact was memorised and then, much later, written down.

Something similar is going on now with the production and publishing of websites, built from the merger of cultural experience with those bits of code that we have been preserving and hoarding at the back of a drawer somewhere in the attic.

Extension

Be careful out there.

references and
further reading

BOOKS AND JOURNALS

Bardini, Thierry (1997) 'Bridging the Gulfs: From Hypertext to Cyberspace', *Journal of Computer-Mediated Communication* (September 1997), http://www.ascusc.org/jcmc/vol3/issue2/bardini.html

Brabazon, Tara (2001) 'How Imagined are Virtual Communities?', *Mots Pluriels* (no. 18, August 2001), http://www.arts.uwa.edu.au/MotsPluriels/ MP1801tb2.html

Crystal, David (1998) *Rediscover Grammar*, Harlow: Longman

Crystal, David (2001) *Language and the Internet*, Cambridge: Cambridge University Press

Fiske, John (1982) *Introduction to Communication Studies*, London: Methuen

Goddard, Angela (2002) *The Language of Advertising: Written texts*, 2nd edn, London: Routledge

Leech, Geoffrey (1983) *Principles of Pragmatics*, Harlow: Longman

McAdams, Mindy and Berger, Stephanie (2001) 'Hypertext', *The Journal of Electronic Publishing* (vol. 6, issue 3, March 2001), http://www.press. umich.edu/jep/06-03/McAdams/pages/

McLuhan, Marshall (2001, [1967]) *Understanding Media* (Routledge Classics), London: Routledge

Shortis, Tim (2001) *The Language of ICT*, London: Routledge

Sterne, Laurence (1967, first published 1759–67), *Tristram Shandy: Life and opinions of Tristram Shandy, Gentleman*, London: Penguin

Strom, David (1995) 'Managing a Web of a Mess', *Infoworld* (12 November 1995), http://www.strom.com/pubwork/iw_web.html

Stubbs, Michael (1983) *Discourse Analysis*, Oxford: Blackwell Publishers

Todorov, Tzvetan (1981) *Introduction to Poetics (Theory and History of Literature)*, trans. P. Brooks, Minneapolis, Minn.: University of Minnesota Press

Whittaker, Jason (2002) *The Internet: The basics*, London: Routledge

Wong, Janine and Storkerson, Peter (1997) 'Hypertext and the Art of Memory', *Visible Language* (31 February 1997), http://www.id.iit.edu/visiblelanguage/Feature_Articles/ArtofMemory/ArtofMemory.html

WEB PUBLICATIONS

Bickmore, Timothy W. (1999) 'Social Intelligence in Conversational Computer Agents', web.media.mit.edu/~bickmore/ProSem/final.pdf

Blood, Rebecca (2000) 'Weblogs: A History and Perspective', http://www.rebeccablood.net/essays/weblog_history.html

Brin, Sergey and Page, Lawrence (1998) 'The Anatomy of a Large-Scale Hypertextual Web Search Engine', gunther.smeal.psu.edu/papers/E-Commerce/355/http:zSzzSzwww.ece.cmu.eduzSz~ece845zSzsp01zSzdocszSz google98.pdf/brin98anatomy.pdf

Chandler, Daniel (1998) 'Personal Home Pages and the Construction of Identities on the Web', http://www.aber.ac.uk/media/Documents/short/webident.html

Chandler, Daniel (2000) 'Biases of the Ear and Eye', http://www.aber.ac.uk/media/Documents/litoral/litoral1.html

Chandler, Daniel and Roberts-Young, Dilwyn (1998) 'The Construction of Identity in the Personal Homepages of Adolescents', http://www.aber.ac.uk/media/Documents/short/strasbourg.html

Cummins, Jean (1997) 'From Mud to Multimedia: The Development of Information Technology within the Graphic Design Industry', http://www.cbltwork.soton.ac.uk/cummins/foun/

Daly, Christopher B. (1998) 'Introduction to Hypertext Writing Style', http://www.bu.edu/cdaly/hyper.html

Douglas, J. Yellowlees 'What Hypertexts Can Do that Print Narratives Cannot', http://www.nwe.ufl.edu/~jdouglas/reader.pdf

Eskelinen, Markku (1997) 'Omission Impossible: The Ergodics of Time', presented at Digital Arts And Culture (26–28 November 1998, Bergen, Norway), http://.cmc.uib.no/dac98/papers/eskelinen.html

Inder, Robert and Oberlander, Jon (1994) 'Applying Discourse Theory to aid Hypertext Navigation', presented at the 1994 European Conference on Hypermedia Technology, http://www.hcrc.ed.ac.uk/gal/Publications/echt94.html

Kilfeather, Eoin (1998) 'Hypertext, Narrative and Coherence: The Role of the Reader and Writer In the Practice of Hypertext', for the award of M.Phil., Dublin Institute of Technology, http://www.dmc.dit.ie/eoin/interview/Hypertext_and_Text61.pdf

Lovink, Geert (2002) 'Principles of Streaming Sovereignty: A History of the Xchange Network', http://www.molodiez.org/net/sound_geert.html

Luo, Vivian (2000) 'Streaming Media: Opportunities and Challenges', http://web.ptc.org/library/proceedings/ptc2000/sessions/monday/m35/m352/

Mancini, Clara (2000) 'From Cinematographic to Hypertext Narrative', http://kmi.open.ac.uk/people/clara/files/tech.rep.pdf

Mancini, Clara and Buckingham Shum, Simon (2001) 'Cognitive Coherence Relations and Hypertext: From Cinematic Patterns to Scholarly Discourse', http://kmi.open.ac.uk/publications/papers/kmi-tr-110.pdf

Mason, Jean S. (2000) 'From Gutenberg's Galaxy to Cyberspace: The Transforming Power of Electronic Hypertext', doctoral dissertation at McGill University, Montréal, http://www.masondissertation.elephanthost.com

Menczer, Filippo (2002) 'Lexical and Semantic Clustering by Web Links', http://www-cse.uta.edu/~alp/ix/readings/lexicalSemanticClustering.pdf

Sorrells, Walter (1995) 'The Heist, A Hypertext Tale', http://www.waltersorrells.com/2.html

Soules, Marshall (2002) 'Animating the Language Machine: Computers and Performance', http://www.mala.bc.ca/~soules/animate.htm

Strehovec, Janez (2004) 'Internet Culture and Internet Textuality', http://razor.arnes.si/~ljzpubs1/theories.htm

Turney, P.D. (2002) 'Mining the Web for Lexical Knowledge to Improve Keyphrase Extraction: Learning from Labeled and Unlabeled Data', http://cogprints.ecs.soton.ac.uk/archive/00002497/01/ERB-1096.pdf

Wallsten, Scott (2003) 'Regulation and Internet Use in Developing Countries', related publication 03-8, AEI-Brookings Joint Center for Regulatory Studies, http://www.aei-brookings.org/admin/authorpdfs/page.php?id=262

index of terms

404 77
The **code** number that appears when you try to access a web page that does not exist, or when your **Internet** connection is not working.

abstract 28
Anything to do with ideas that do not have physical form. 'Life' is an abstract noun.

adjacency pair 50
Pairs of utterances in a conversation that go together through habit or **convention**. 'How are you?' will often be followed by 'Fine'.

adjectival 61
This means relating to an adjective. However, it is sometimes used to describe a class other than an adjective when it is used as a modifier. For example, 'dog collar' where 'dog' is a noun but is used adjectivally.

adjective cluster 60
A string of adjectives that **pre-modify** the head of a noun phrase, as in 'big green resplendent fish' where three adjectives form a cluster.

ameliorate 47
A word is said to undergo amelioration when it gains a more favourable meaning through the passage of time, so that 'rogue' is

now a relatively mild insult. **Pragmatic** factors, such as context and cultural assumptions, can also ameliorate the impact of an utterance.

analogue 5
A way of storing and representing information where the recording and playback system tries to copy or reproduce the original, without trying to select out significant parts. A vinyl record is an analogue of the original music it simulates.

anaphoric reference 63
A grammatical device where, commonly, a pronoun refers back to a noun or noun phrase from a previous sentence. For example: 'John has gone shopping. He will not be long.'

anchorage 48
Where one element of a **media text** is used to pin down and specify the meaning of another part of the **text**. Captions are said to 'anchor' the meaning of photographs in newspapers.

antonym 75
A word that means the opposite of another word.

artificial intelligence 83
The area of computer science that strives to make computer systems mimic the workings of the human brain.

asynchronous 40
Literally means 'not happening at the same time'. Refers to a communication system where the sender and the receiver are not taking part at the same time. Email is asynchronous, whereas telephone conversations are **synchronous**.

author 34
To author, used as a verb, means to construct **hypertext** systems such as **websites** or CD-ROM **software**.

backbone 39
A very high speed **Internet** link, often owned by an Internet service provider. So-called because the lower speed links that join on to it are supposed to resemble ribs emanating from a spine.

bandwidth 61
The volume of **data** that an **Internet** link is capable of carrying, and how fast it can carry that data. This is the origin of the term '**broadband**', which has become **synonymous** with high speed Internet access.

blocked 14
In paragraph formatting, where there is no **indent** on the first line and paragraph breaks are indicated by inserting an extra line of **white space** between paragraphs.

blog 48
A web-based personal diary – short for '**weblog**'.

body text 13
The **text** that forms the principal content of a printed page or web page. Sometimes refers to the **typeface** and layout used for this content.

Boolean logic 84
A logic used in many computer programming languages, in which expressions and conditions can be combined using operators like 'AND', 'OR' and 'NOT', enabling complex instructions to be given to computers without ambiguity.

branding 18
The association of a word, phrase, logo, picture or piece of music (or any combination of these) with the public perception of a product or service. Usually a conscious creation on the part of advertisers or marketing professionals.

broadband 20
An **Internet** connection capable of carrying large amounts of **data** at very high speeds. It began to replace **modem** access for home users in the early twenty-first century. *See* **bandwidth**.

browser 10
Software used to **download** and display copies of web pages on **personal computers**.

buffered 56
When **data** is **downloaded** and stored in a temporary memory area, so that it can be used to keep the data flow going if the connection or data stream is interrupted: the buffer begins to empty, and the device attempts to get the connection back before the data in the buffer runs out.

bug 6
An unforeseen error in programming, which causes **software** to behave in a way that has not been predicted.

cached 79
    When a copy of a web page is
    stored on a local computer, so that
    the page can be accessed more
    quickly next time, it is described
    as being cached. The system has to
    be designed so that only an up-to-
    date copy is kept.

character 88
    Originally an element of written
    language (a letter in the alphabet),
    it came to be used for the letters
    and symbols on a keyboard, and
    then for the unique **code** that
    each key generates.

clause 19
    A verb or verb combination that
    forms the smallest possible unit of
    a sentence.

client 107
    A computer that requests and
    downloads data from a **server**.

code 4
    The hidden language that lies
    beneath the appearance of a web
    page. The code is a set of
    instructions for the **browser**.

coded 90
    The term used for a web page
    when it has been prepared for
    uploading to a site. Often this
    coding is done by professionals
    who are familiar with how to
    achieve effects using raw **HTML**.
    Amateurs will often use a
    WYSIWYG editor to generate the
    required **code**.

complement 28
    Some verbs take an adjective
    after them instead of a noun.
    This adjective is known as a
    complement rather than an **object**.
    For example, 'It seems old' where
    'old' is the complement.

compounding 61
    The joining together of two words
    to make a new word.

compressed 56
    When **data** has **redundant**
    information stripped out, and
    then the significant data is
    rearranged to take up less disk
    space, it is said to be compressed.
    Compressed data is not usually
    readable without first
    uncompressing it.

concrete 28
    Usually refers to a noun that
    describes a physically tangible
    object or living being.

conditional 78
    Often refers to a **sub-clause** that
    describes a condition which has to
    be met before the event in the
    main clause can happen. It is
    usually preceded by the word 'if'.
    For example: 'If you give me some
    money, I will go into town.'

configure 13
    To alter settings in either
    hardware or **software**.

context of reception 11
    The physical situation in which
    the **text** is read.

convention 4
    In general, a convention is an
    accepted way of doing something.
    In linguistic, literary and media
    analysis it refers to established
    ways of constructing a **text** that is
    closely linked to audience
    expectations.

coordinating conjunction 19
    A word that joins two **clauses**, but
    gives each of the two clauses equal
    grammatical status. The main one

in English is 'and', as in 'She watches television and she falls asleep'.

co-present 42
Refers to a context in which the sender and the recipient of the **text** are physically present – **synchronous** communication. With **electronic** texts, the notion of co-presence does not necessarily imply that the participants are present in the same physical space – only that they are participating in the same live communicative act.

crash 61
This is the term used when a computer ceases to function, in its designated way, usually without warning. The usual cause is incompatibility between different **software** packages and/or the impossibility of predicting how the software will behave with every conceivable **hardware configuration**.

cyclic narrative 19
Most **narratives** are **linear**, in that they imitate the passage of time and depict a causal universe where one event leads to another.
A cyclic or circular narrative is an experimental type which ends where it began. Quentin Tarantino's film *Pulp Fiction* and Richard Kelly's film *Donnie Darko* are examples.

data 9
A word meaning 'information'. Specifically, it refers to information that is processed and handled by computers, but its meaning has **widened** beyond this to include any kind of systematically stored information – especially statistical information.

database 19
A store of information kept and processed by a computer. Also refers to the **software** that handles this information, and more recently has come to be used for a store of information not maintained on a computer.

date line 13
The line near the top of the front page of a newspaper that contains the date.

dead links 72
Web **hyperlinks** that lead nowhere, usually because the page that the hyperlink formerly linked to has been deleted from the **server**.

deictic 42
Deictic words make references to immediate context, which cannot always be understood unless you know something about that context. For example, in the utterance 'Pass me that will you?' the word 'that' is a deictic.

demonstrative 60
A demonstrative pronoun is one that provides some kind of **deictic** reference.

Design View 91
In web **authoring software** (HTML editors), Design View is the preview of how the web page will appear when displayed on the **Internet**.

desktop 8
A metaphorical representation of the top of a desk that has dominated computer-user-interface design since the 1970s.

desktop publishing 88

A **software**-based system for professional document design. It first entered the newspaper industry in the early 1980s, but the power and storage capacity of modern home PCs are now more than adequate for running professional DTP software at home.

dialectal 5

The most useful definition of a dialect is that it is marked by lexical and grammatical differences from the standard version of the language. Differences of accent are purely phonetic or phonological.

dial-up 20

A method of accessing the **Internet** that uses standard telephone lines via a device called a **modem**.

digital 6

A way of storing and representing information where the significant parts of the **data** are selected out and translated into numbers (digits) capable of being processed by a computer.

discourse 5

Usually refers to the overall structural organisation of a **text** – structural analysis above the level of the sentence.

domain name 30

A unique computer name that identifies a web **server** – the web address. The domain name is usually the part after the 'www', although increasingly the 'www' part of the address is not required, so that entering just 'microsoft.com' will get you to their **website**.

domain name branding 29

Where a **website** is known by the lexically significant part of its web address, and a conscious effort is made to market the site in this way. An example would be 'www.tesco.com'.

Domain Name Server (DNS) 29

A dedicated **server** that links **IP addresses** to web addresses, so that when you type the address of a **website** into your **browser**, the page you want can be retrieved from the right web server. Each web server has a unique name and a unique IP address.

download 13

To copy a **file** from a remote computer on to your own.

dynamic verb 15

A verb that can be used in the progressive aspect, usually with an '-ing' ending. For example: 'He is climbing the ladder.'

e-book 34

A book that is made available in an **electronic** form, to be read on a computer screen rather than on paper.

Edit View 91

In web **authoring software** (**HTML** editors), Edit View is where the author can enter and alter the HTML **code** directly.

electronic 6

Designed using technology based on the **transistor**, and generally using small, complex circuits with very low voltages. The circuits are commonly used for controlling other systems. To be distinguished from the term 'electrical', which refers to heavier duty systems supplied by mains voltage.

enigma 14

Literally means something that is puzzling, but in **narrative** theory is sometimes used to mean the central mystery that drives the story forward – because the audience want to know the outcome.

environment 8

The **software** infrastructure that allows other software applications to run; very similar in usage to 'operating system'.

exchange 59

A conversational interaction that involves two or more people and has an identifiable structure. It will often involve **adjacency pairs**.

exophoric reference 75

When a **text** refers to other texts outside of itself. The way in which this reference is made can be grammatical, lexical or in terms of imitating the **form** or content of another text.

face 49

In some types of analysis of politeness, the concept of face is divided into positive and negative – where positive face is our desire to be liked and negative face is our desire to be left alone and not have our personal space intruded upon.

fansite 41

A **website** dedicated to the recording and celebration of the activities and achievements of a band, an actor or other phenomenon promoted by the mass media.

file 9

A package of **data** that a computer is capable of storing for later use. **Software** allows files to be named, moved, copied and deleted.

file extension 88

The three (or sometimes four) letters after the dot in a **filename** that denote the type of **file**. For example, 'doc' after the dot indicates that a file is a Microsoft Word file.

filename 30

The name given to a **file** when it is saved to disk.

filter-style 48

A type of **blog** that is basically a collection of links to other **websites**.

floppy disk 55

A removable magnetic disk used for backing up **files** or transferring files between computers. In the very early days of PCs, floppy disks were the sole means of storing **data**.

font 13

Technically, this means the **typeface**, the size and the style (bold, italic) of the print, but computer use has shifted its means to be **synonymous** with 'typeface'.

force 46

As differentiated from '**sense**', this is used in pragmatics to mean the hidden, encultured meaning behind an utterance. So, the utterance 'Are you going to stand there all day?' is not a request for information: it has the **pragmatic** force of trying to make somebody move.

foregrounded 19

When an element of a **text** is foregrounded, it is flagged as being significant. For example, a newspaper editorial foregrounds the opinions of the editor and will usually also foreground its own use of persuasive language – unlike an advertisement, which may foreground references to the product but may want to keep its persuasive strategies hidden.

form 5

Any aspect of the way a **text** is put together. In novels, chapter length is an aspect of form. In films, camera techniques are an aspect of form. Also encompasses concepts like **genre**.

frameworks 1

Related lists of technical terms used in analytical descriptions for the purposes of academic study.

free morphemes 61

Are **morphemes** that can exist outside of the word. For example, the noun 'bookcase' consists of two free morphemes. Morphemes that cannot exist outside the word are called bound morphemes. The morphemes 'un' and 'ful' in 'unhelpful' are examples of this.

freeware 91

Software that is distributed without charge.

functional shift 61

When a word that belongs to a specific word class becomes usable in an additional word class. For example, in the noun 'action' can now also be used as a verb.

gatekeeper 49

A role that involves the monitoring and regulation of the flow of information in and out of an institution.

genitive 60

The form of the noun that indicates possession. In the phrase 'John's house' the noun 'John' is in the genitive form.

genre 41

Type of **text** that is defined by audience expectations of the **conventions** it should use.

graphical 4

Refers to elements of a **text** that are purely pictorial or included for visual aesthetic effect.

graphology 10

A **framework** that allows textual analysis focused on how the forms of the **characters** (letters) affect the relationship between **text** and audience.

handwriting font 47

A **font** (or **typeface**) that tries to imitate the letter shapes of handwriting.

hard disk 55

A permanently installed disk inside the computer where **software file**s and **data** files are stored.

hardware 26

The physical **electronic** components of the computer system, as distinct from **software** – a set of instructions to make the computer perform its main functions, loaded while the computer is switched on but having no physical existence when it is switched off.

hard-wired 8

Encoded or determined by the physical **electronic** wiring of the system, as opposed to **software** – which is only loaded for a transient period while the computer is switched on. Software has the advantage that it can be updated easily, whereas hard-wired systems can only be updated by the physical replacement of **hardware**.

hit 25

A web address that appears as part of list of pages resulting from a search engine query. Can also refer to the accessing of a web page: some **webmasters** keep a record of how many hits a page has received, either for marketing purposes or for managing the amount of traffic the site receives.

home page 37

The **web presence** for an organisation or person, closely linked to the identity of that organisation or person.

hosted 29

Kept on a web **server**.

house style 14

The combination of **text** and graphics that forms part of the **brand** image of an institution. Can refer to any kind of document – paper-based or **electronic**.

hover button 25

A graphic that changes as the mouse is moved over it.

HTML 14

Hypertext Mark-up Language – the programming language used to create web pages.

hyperlink 10

Part of a web page that enables the reader to jump to another web page by clicking on it with the mouse.

hyper-narrative 31

Narrative that has its structure and **conventions** determined by its existence in a **hypertext environment**.

hyperspace 40

The metaphorical space occupied by interlinked **hypertext** documents. When you are surfing the Web, you are in hyperspace.

hypertext 9

Electronic text in which documents are linked together with **hyperlinks**.

Hypertext Transfer Protocol 29

The method used to move copies of web pages from **servers** to web **browsers**.

idiomatic 75

When the meaning of a specific word or phrase is culturally determined and is therefore usually peculiar to one language. For example, the phrase 'pass the buck' is an Anglo-American idiom that would not translate successfully into other languages.

indented 14

In paragraph formatting, where the start of a new paragraph is indicated by starting the first line further way from the left margin than the rest of the **text**.

Internet 9

A global **network** of computers.

Internet Service Provider (ISP) 30
A company that sells access to the **Internet**, in the same way as other companies sell access to utilities like gas and electricity.

intertextuality 31
When a **text** makes a reference to another text – either explicitly or implicitly.

intonation 4
Variation in **pitch** throughout the length of an utterance, often carrying **pragmatic** meaning. For example, if the pitch rises at the end of an utterance it can turn the utterance into a question.

intranet 36
A web-based **network** that provides web pages and **websites** for private consumption only. Access is usually restricted to members of an organisation (such as a company or a school) and cannot be viewed from the wider **Internet** without a password.

IP address 103
A unique number that identifies every computer on the **Internet** or on a **LAN**, whether it is a **server** or a **client**. When a PC connects to the Internet, it is given a temporary IP address. The IP address of this laptop is currently 192.168.0.128.

lexeme 30
The smallest unit of language that has a meaning and refers to a distinct cultural concept.

lexical cohesion 11
The way in which a **text** hangs together through repeated patterns of words.

linear 15
Moving in a line. Used to describe **narrative** structure when it does

not involve jumping backwards and forwards in time.

Linotype 93
A machine designed to automate the typesetting process in newspaper production. A highly complex machine to operate, which could take years of training in its use. Made redundant by the advent of **digital** document processing in the early 1980s.

Local Area Network (LAN) 9
A group of computers linked together in a building or complex of buildings. Used for sharing **software** and **data files**, but not (or not primarily) intended to be accessible by the outside world.

Macintosh 10
This refers to the so-called 'Apple Mac' **personal computers**. They pre-date the type of PC that was eventually to run Microsoft Windows. Apple Macs are still around today, and have their own **operating system** (MacOS) which is not related in a technical way to Windows. They are most widely used in professional publishing, graphic design and video editing.

macro 93
A set of instructions designed to automate a process in a **software** package. Macros are written in languages that resemble programming languages.
An example of a macro would be an extra menu item in Microsoft Word (added by the installation of the macro) that could check the spelling in a document and then copy all the misspelled words into a new document.

107

Macromedia Flash 59

A **software plug-in** for web **browsers** that enables web developers to include animated graphics as part of a **website**.

mainframe 9

A large computer set up to focus on raw processing power rather than running user-friendly **software**. Mainframes can be accessed remotely, using a dedicated terminal or a PC **configured** to act as a terminal.

masthead 14

The area on the front page of a newspaper or magazine that contains the **title** of the publication in its characteristic **font**, with associated colour and **graphical** elements.

match 76

Similar to a **hit**, this means the address of a page which appears to hold the keywords used in a particular search engine query.

media text 59

Media theory defines a **text** in a much broader sense than either linguistic or literary study. It basically means any coherently structured expression, transmitted by the mass media, that shows evidence of using media **conventions**. So, a television advertisement and a billboard poster would both be media texts.

medium 10

Means of transmitting a message. A medium that reaches a large audience is called a mass medium. The Web is one of the newest mass media. It is in a category called 'new media', so called because they make use of **digital**, **electronic** technology in unprecedented ways.

merchandising 59

The production, marketing and sale of products associated with a **text** such as a cinema film or a television show. A common example would be the sale of action figures and clothing related to the characters in a film.

microchip 69

A miniaturised, **transistor**-based circuit that made the **personal computer** possible technologically.

mnemonic 49

Something which acts to stimulate memory.

modal verb 78

A verb appearing before the main verb in a sentence, which tends to indicate some aspect of possibility or obligation. For example, in the sentence 'We must watch TV', the verb 'must' is modal. Modal verbs do not have past or present tense, and they do not change form according to the person or number of the **subject**.

modem 13

A device used to gain access to the **Internet** using a standard (voice) telephone line (**dial-up** access).

modernist 49

Modernism was a movement in the creative arts, and in academic thinking in general that began in the early twentieth century. Modernist writers and artists attempted to **foreground** the nature of human experience and perception by experimenting with **form**.

monospaced 13

A **typeface** where the letters do not vary in width.

morpheme 30

Part of a word. There are bound and **free morphemes** (see above), and there are also grammatical and lexical morphemes. A lexical morpheme conveys meaning, whereas a grammatical morpheme only has a grammatical function. So the morpheme 'ed' on 'climbed' has no lexical meaning, but its function is to give the verb past meaning.

morpho-lexical 30

A linguistic feature that is a mixture of **morphology** and lexis. For example, the segment 'un' on the front of an adjective (as in 'unhelpful') has a morphological relationship with the rest of the word, but also some lexical meaning in its own right ('the opposite of').

morphology 109

Grammatical relationships between parts of a word (**morphemes**).

motif 18

Similar in use to the word 'theme', a motif is a repeated image or idea that characterises a particular **media text**.

multimedia 53

Refers to a device, a **media text** or even simply an experience that combines sound, **text**, graphics and images – especially moving images. In the 1990s, the term became associated with CD-ROM-based **software**.

narrative 3

In simple terms, a narrative is a story; but in media and literary theory it refers to the way the story is structured, and to the study of generic types that underlie all stories.

neologism 61

A newly invented word.

networking 9

Linking computers together so that they can share **files** and resources such as printers. The **Internet** is one giant computer network.

node 15

Component part of a **hypertext** system that contains links to other nodes. A web page is a typical hypertext node.

nominal 61

A word that performs a naming function. It is a wider, more **notional** term than 'noun' because it includes words that are not nouns – 'running', for example.

non-finite 58

In reference to a **clause** or verb, this indicates that it is not governed by a **subject**. Usually either the 'to' or the '-ing' form of a verb. So, 'eating' and 'to eat' are non-finite forms.

notional 42

A notional concept is one that is arrived at through intuition or common sense, and therefore a concept that cannot be proven through formal criteria or logic. The idea that a verb is a 'doing word' is notional, because it can be argued that many 'doing words'

are not verbs. For example,
'activity' is a doing word but it
is a noun.

object 15
As a grammatical function – the
noun or noun phrase that is on
the receiving end of an action
performed by a verb. So, in the
sentence 'John reads his red book',
the noun phrase 'his red book' is
the object.

offline 57
Not connected to the **Internet**.
Applies more to a **dial-up**
connection where you might be
using the only phone line in the
house or paying for your time
online. In this situation, email
messages would usually be
composed offline and then you
would go online to send them.

online 18
Connected to the **Internet**.

operating system 8
The **environment** in which
software runs. The most famous
example is Microsoft Windows.
An operating system tries to be
user-friendly by representing itself
as an extended metaphor of
something from the physical
world – the virtual **desktop**, for
example.

packet 9
A segment of **data** transmitted
over a computer **network**.

page caching 79
The practice whereby search
engines keep copies of external
web pages on their own **servers**
so that the process of searching
is speeded up.

park 30
To reserve an **Internet domain
name** until the owner of the
domain name develops some
content to include on their
website. This service is usually
offered by web **hosting**
companies.

participle 33
In English, a form of the verb that
indicates whether an action is
completed or ongoing. Present
participles have the ending '-ing'
whereas most past participles have
the ending '-ed', as in the
examples 'She is stopping' and
'She has stopped'.

passive 77
A sentence type where the **subject**
of the sentence is the **object** or
person on the receiving end of the
action. For example: 'The ball was
hit by the girl.'

persona 50
A constructed, fictional person
who, for example, is the imagined
voice behind the **narrative** in a
novel. The term also provides the
critical distance needed to avoid
thinking of fictional characters as
real people.

personal computer 1
Developed originally as a
miniaturised and more user-
friendly version of a **mainframe**
computer, the PC has now come
to be what most people have in
mind when they say 'computer'.
First marketed by Apple in the
1970s, the term PC has now also
means IBM-compatible computers
in the open architecture model
that have saturated the market
since the late 1980s.

pitch 4
> Determined by length and
> tautness of vocal cords, this refers
> to how high or low the 'note' of
> the human voice is.

plain text 88
> **Text** without formatting
> characteristics such as **font** style,
> bold and italic.

platform 56
> Can refer to the kind of computer
> a **software** package is running on
> (for example, PC or Apple Mac).
> Sometimes refers to the **operating
> system** (**environment**) – such as
> Windows or MacOS.

plug-in 26
> A small piece of **software** that
> extends the capabilities of a web
> **browser**. The **Macromedia Flash**
> plug-in enables a web browser to
> play animations built using the
> Macromedia Flash **authoring**
> software.

pop-up window 62
> A reduced size **browser** window
> that appears spontaneously when
> you visit certain **websites** or run
> certain **software**. Usually used for
> unsolicited advertising.

portal 28
> A **website** that offers to be a
> gateway to the rest of the Web.
> Includes, for example, search
> engines, subject-related groups of
> links, news, games, web-based
> email services and advertising.
> Well-known examples are MSN
> and Yahoo.

post-modernist 49
> As well as experimenting with
> **form**, post-modernism seeks to
> question the nature of human

experience and our perceptions of
reality.

post-modified 24
> A noun phrase in which the
> modifier comes after the head, as
> in 'the book on the table', where
> 'on the table' is the modifier.

pragmatic 3
> Pragmatic meaning is hidden,
> **subtextual** meaning determined
> by cultural and contextual factors.
> It is very often nothing to do with
> the linguistic form or literal **sense**
> of the words. For example, the
> phrase 'Don't put all your eggs in
> one basket' is unlikely to have any
> meaning at all if translated into
> other languages.

prefix 60
> A **morpheme** that goes before the
> main (lexical) morpheme in a
> word. An example is 'dis', which
> can change the meaning of some
> verbs, e.g. 'displace', 'disobey'.

pre-modified 76
> A noun phrase that is modified,
> usually by determiners and
> adjectives, before the head, as in
> 'the small black book'.

processor 54
> The **microchip** that performs all
> of the computer's numerical
> calculations. Everything that the
> computer does is reduced to a
> numerical calculation, so that the
> processor is often considered the
> brain of the computer.

programmer 7
> Someone who creates computer
> **software**.

proportionally spaced 13
> A **typeface** in which the **charac-
> ters** (letters) are of varying width.

pull quote 15

A short extract from an article, often reported speech, that is meant to have instant impact and sum up the overall content of the article. Pull quotes can appear underneath the headline of the article, or be used inside **white space** to visually break up a column of print.

QWERTY keyboard 8

The keyboard layout that became the standard for the manual typewriter.

RAM 62

Random Access Memory. The area where the computer stores **data** temporarily. It does this because data can be retrieved from memory much more quickly than it can from disk. The more RAM a computer has, the faster it will run.

reader stance 11

The metaphorical position that the reader occupies in relation to the **text**, and consequently how the text is decoded and received. Can be determined by factors such as the sociocultural background of the reader and the physical and/or emotional context in which the text is received. Similar to the term 'positioning' in media studies.

real time 56

If a **narrative** takes place in real time, it does not use **compression**, so the events take as long to unfold on the screen as they would in real life. A recent example of experimenting with real-time narrative is the television drama series '24'.

redundancy 56

Any information or **data**, in a **text**, that is not essential for the basic information to come across. So, from a communication studies perspective, a poem will contain a great deal of redundancy, whereas a recipe will contain a great deal less. The term can also refer to the duplication of essential **electronic** systems, so that the duplicate takes over in the event of a failure. Aeroplane control systems contain this kind of redundancy.

register 23

The degree of formality of a **text**, determined by the socially accepted requirements of its context.

relativiser 78

A word that introduces a relative **clause** in a sentence. So, in the sentence 'I saw the girl who broke the window', the word 'who' is a relativiser.

rich text 13

Text that contains formatting attributes such as **typeface**, bold and italic.

root 74

The lexically significant part of a noun or verb, without endings to signify number or tense.

rotating banner advertisement 18

An advertisement that appears usually near the top of a web page, where the content of the advertisement changes at regular intervals – in a similar way to an **electronic** billboard. The advertisement is normally a **hyperlink**, so that you can click on it to learn more about or buy the product or service.

sans serif 13

A family of **typefaces** without **serifs** (flourishes at the ends of the ascenders and descenders). The most well-known of these is Arial, which has been popularised by its installation as one of the default typefaces in Microsoft Windows.

search dialogue 19

A dialogue is a box that the computer presents you with, requiring the input of **text** or the selection of an option using the mouse; so a search dialogue is asking you what you want to search for.

semantic 3

Anything related to word meaning, and how these meanings relate to each other.

semiology

See **semiotics**.

semiotics 47

The interpretation of **texts** and other communicative acts, using the concept of the sign. A sign consists of a signifier and a signified. The signifier could be a word, in the case of language, or a close-up of an object, in the case of film; the signified is the object or concept that the signifier refers to. So, the sign 'love' consists of the word combined with our mental impression of what love is. Note that semiotic systems are very much culturally determined, so that the verb 'aimer' has multiple meanings for a French audience – meanings that its English translation does not possess.

sense 75

As opposed to **force**, in pragmatics, sense is the literal meaning of an utterance. So, the sense of the utterance 'Are you going to stand there all day?' is a request of information about the person's intended movements.

serif 13

Flourishes (usually tapered) on the ends of ascenders and descenders in some **typefaces**. Also the name given to that family of typefaces.

server 29

A computer on a **network**, dedicated to performing functions such as the sharing of **files** or **software**. A web server is dedicated to storing copies of web pages and delivering copies of them to web **browsers** on **personal computers**.

sidebar 18

Originally a story appearing at the side of the main front page story in a newspaper, giving a different perspective on that story. In web page design, a coloured area at the side of the page that typically contains categorised links to the content of the site.

site clustering 79

In search engine query results, the practice of grouping **hits** from the same site together as **indented** lists. Prevents the query results from being filled with hits that are all from the same site.

site map 31

A simplified, sometimes diagrammatic, representation of the **hypertext** structure of the entire **website**.

slab serif 28

A development of **serif typefaces**, in which the serif is either not tapered or only very slightly tapered.

small caps 28
A typographical attribute in which all the **characters** are in upper-case form, but the non-capitals are differentiated by making them smaller.

SMS text messaging 18
Plain text content with a limit of 160 **characters** per message, sent between mobile phone handsets (SMS stands for Short Message Service.)

socialised 29
Conditioned to behave within the accepted practices of a social group.

sociolinguistic 74
Refers to the ways in which social factors such as ethnicity and gender affect language **form** and language function.

software 7
A set of instructions for a computer, written by a **programmer**, that turn the computer into a dedicated tool for doing a particular job – handling documents or storing complex records, for example.

sound card 55
A **hard-wired** device for enabling a computer to make sounds through an external amplifier and speakers. Part of a computer's **multimedia** capability.

streaming media 19
Sound and video content delivered via a **website**. Instead of delivering a copy of the **data** all at once, the data is fed continuously in a live stream, and some of it is buffered by the receiving computer in case of errors in the stream.

sub-clause 61
A **clause** that is grammatically less important than the main clause. In the sentence 'The book which I discovered was interesting' the clause 'which I discovered' is a sub-clause.

sub-editing 20
Adjusting the word count, stylistic consistency, spelling, grammar and overall sense of a journalist's article copy, and preparing its layout for final publication.

subject 28
The noun or noun phrase in sentence that governs the verb. So, the sentence 'They make bread' has 'They' as the subject, but if the subject was 'He' the verb form would have to change to 'makes'.

subject-verb 58
The simplest possible sentence type in English. For example: 'She walks.'

subtext 26
Similar to **pragmatic** meaning: any encoded message that not explicit in the **form** of the **text**. In a novel, for example, the subtext would not be openly stated in the **narrative** but would be apparent in the actions of the characters.

symbolic 4
Symbolism involves a cultural agreement about what certain signs represent (*see* **semiotics**). For example, the colour blue often symbolises peace and tranquillity.

synchronous 48
A form of communication where both the sender and receiver of

the message are physically present or virtually present (as in a chatroom).

synonymous 75
Synonymy is a **semantic** relationship where a group of words mean the same as each other.

syntagmatic 49
The relationship between parts of a sequence. For example, how the **subject** relates to the verb in a sentence is a syntagmatic relationship, as is the editing together of a sequence of shots to be used in the **title** sequence of a film.

Syntax 24
Grammatical relationships between words in a sentence.

system requirements 26
The minimum level of **hardware** a computer needs in order to run a piece of **software**. Usually refers to **processor** speed, **RAM** size and **hard disk** space.

tag 88
An instruction to the web **browser** about aspects of **text** formatting, graphics and **hyperlinks**. Enclosed in special brackets, so that the browser can tell the difference between tags and textual content.

tagline 62
A short phrase used in the marketing of a film, in order to sum up the content of the film and attract potential audiences. Often included as part of the official poster advertising the film.

teletext 65
A **text**-based information service carried by television signals and readable on suitably equipped TV sets. Digital TV signals now carry a much more **graphical** form of teletext which shares some of the **hypertextual** features of the Web.

text 1
From the outset, this book uses the wider definition of a text – encompassing what are often referred to as **media texts**.

text editor 88
Software designed for editing **plain text files**. Often used by **HTML** developers for creating and editing web pages at raw HTML **code** level.

title 75
An **HTML tag** that makes a short description of the web page appear in the blue bar at the top of your **browser** window.

Todorov, Tzvetan 14
A **narrative** theorist who developed the stability-threat-resolution model. This model attempts to account for most stories in terms of a central problem or **enigma**, creating a motivational structure in which the audience continue reading or watching in order to see the resolution of the problem.

toolbar 62
A strip of icons, usually across the top of the **software** window, which provide short cuts to commonly used menu items.

transistor 6

A simple miniaturised amplifier component that forms the basis of modern **electronic** circuits.

transitional marker 46

A stylistic device which signals to the reader that the **text** is about to change direction in some way, perhaps dealing with a new topic or shifting its time reference – a visual disturbance leading into a flashback, for example.

typeface 13

A design concept for printed **characters**, where consistent stylistic features are applied to all the characters.

unregulated 24

In most countries, the mass media are regulated by legal constraints on the content of **media texts** and ownership of media organisations. Although the Web is subject to more regulation than it used to be, the technical infrastructure of the Web still means that national boundaries are not really significant and a **website** that was shut down in one country can re-emerge in another and still be visible globally. Media regulation in the traditional sense is impossible.

upload 36

Transfer a copy of a **file** from your computer to a remote computer.

URL 11

Uniform Resource Locator – a **website** address.

variety 5

In **sociolinguistics**, a way of communicating that can be isolated according to formal linguistic criteria and then linked to a social factor such as region or ethnicity. For example, an accent is a variety that can be seen to contain pronunciation features that only occur in a defined geographical area. A dialect is a variety defined by grammatical and lexical features.

verb phrase 15

The group of words in a sentence that fulfils the verb function. For example, in the sentence 'Jane had been looking sad' the phrase 'had been looking' is the verb phrase.

verb tense 15

A change in the form of a verb, usually linked to a time reference. In English, adding '-ed' to most verbs makes them past tense.

weblog 42

A web-based diary or journal, with formal characteristics of its own.

webmaster 106

The person responsible for maintaining a **website**.

web presence 10

Usually just means the **website** maintained by an organisation or an individual. Also carries the added association of how an organisation markets its image via the Web.

website 1

A collection of interlinked web pages, maintained at the same **URL**. The collection has a coherent structure, centred on a default page, and is usually attempting to promote the identity of an organisation or person, both in terms of style and content.

white space 18
A typographical **convention** whereby areas of empty paper, containing no print, provide visual clues about textual organisation.

Wide Area Network (WAN) 9
A computer **network** covering a large geographical area. Can consist of a series of interlinked **LANs** (see above). The **Internet** is an example of a WAN.

widen 60
A **semantic** process whereby a word gains more lexical meanings than it had previously. An example would be 'stress', which, in the past twenty years, has come to mean any kind of psychological pressure created by any aspect of modern living. This originates from a much narrower medical definition of the word.

word processing 6
Using **software** designed to manage, edit and print **electronic** copies of typed documents.